THE ALASKA PURCHASE IN AMERICAN HISTORY

Other titles *in American History*

The Alamo
in American History
(ISBN 0-89490-770-0)

The Alaska Purchase
in American History
(ISBN 0-7660-1138-0)

Alcatraz Prison
in American History
(ISBN 0-89490-990-8)

The Battle of the Little Bighorn
in American History
(ISBN 0-89490-768-9)

The Boston Tea Party
in American History
(ISBN 0-7660-1139-9)

The California Gold Rush
in American History
(ISBN 0-89490-878-2)

The Fight for Women's
Right to Vote
in American History
(ISBN 0-89490-986-X)

The Great Depression
in American History
(ISBN 0-89490-881-2)

The Industrial Revolution
in American History
(ISBN 0-89490-985-1)

Japanese-American Internment
in American History
(ISBN 0-89490-767-0)

John Brown's Raid
on Harpers Ferry
in American History
(ISBN 0-7660-1123-2)

Lewis and Clark's
Journey of Discovery
in American History
(ISBN 0-7660-1127-5)

The Lincoln Assassination
in American History
(ISBN 0-89490-886-3)

McCarthy and the
Fear of Communism
in American History
(ISBN 0-89490-987-8)

The Mormon Trail
and the Latter-day Saints
in American History
(ISBN 0-89490-988-6)

Native Americans and the
Reservation in American History
(ISBN 0-89490-769-7)

The Oregon Trail
in American History
(ISBN 0-89490-771-9)

The Panama Canal
in American History
(ISBN 0-7660-1216-6)

Reconstruction Following
the Civil War
in American History
(ISBN 0-7660-1140-2)

The Salem Witchcraft Trials
in American History
(ISBN 0-7660-1125-9)

Slavery and Abolition
in American History
(ISBN 0-7660-1124-0)

The Transcontinental Railroad
in American History
(ISBN 0-89490-882-0)

The Underground Railroad
in American History
(ISBN 0-89490-885-5)

The Watergate Scandal
in American History
(ISBN 0-89490-883-9)

IN
AMERICAN
HISTORY

THE ALASKA PURCHASE IN AMERICAN HISTORY

David K. Fremon

Enslow Publishers, Inc.

40 Industrial Road	PO Box 38
Box 398	Aldershot
Berkeley Heights, NJ 07922	Hants GU12 6BP
USA	UK

http://www.enslow.com

Dedicated to Grandma, Mike, and Ann

Library of Congress Cataloging-in-Publication Data

Fremon, David K.
    The Alaska Purchase in American history / David K. Fremon.
        p.   cm. — (In American history)
    Includes bibliographical references and index.
    Summary: Traces the history of Alaska through the Russian exploration
and settlement to the American purchase of the territory by William
Seward in 1867, discussing key personalities and events during this
period.
    ISBN 0-7660-1138-0
    1. Alaska—Annexation to the United States—Juvenile literature.
2. Alaska—History—To 1867—Juvenile literature. 3. Russians—
Alaska—History—Juvenile literature. [1. Alaska—History—To 1867.
2. Russians—Alaska—History. 3. Alaska—Annexation to the United
States.] I. Title. II. Series.
F907.F74   1999
979.8—dc21   98-48913
                                                         CIP
                                                          AC

Printed in the United States of America

10 9 8 7 6 5 4 3 2

To Our Readers:
All Internet addresses in this book were active and appropriate when we
went to press. Any comments or suggestions can be sent by e-mail to
Comments@enslow.com or to the address on the back cover.

Illustration Credits: Alaska State Library, pp. 15, 16, 18, 23, 49, 88,
114; David K. Fremon, pp. 45, 109; Enslow Publishers, Inc., pp. 12, 32;
Library of Congress, pp. 38, 44, 63, 69, 78, 83, 89, 98, 101, 103, 107.

Cover Illustrations: Library of Congress; David K. Fremon.

★ CONTENTS ★

"WE NOW STOOD ON AMERICAN SOIL"

United States General Lowell Rousseau stepped into a rowboat from the American ship *Ossipee*. Russian Captain Aleksei Pestchouroff would soon join him at the shore of Sitka's harbor. In a few hours, these two men would represent their nations in a historic exchange.

Captain Pestchouroff was ready to give up a land that the Russians called Russian America and some natives called Alaska. It was a fur hunting and trading center at the northwestern edge of the North American continent. The Russians had hunted fur-bearing sea mammals, such as sea otters and fur seals, to near extinction. Their main source of income was declining, and they had decided to get rid of the colony.

What would Americans do once they took over this gigantic territory? That question remained unsettled. Not everyone in the United States favored buying this unknown land, even if it did cost only two cents an acre. Some gave it nicknames such as "Seward's Folly"—a distant, frozen, inhospitable land bought by foolish Secretary of State William Seward. The House of Representatives had not even approved the money necessary to complete the sale.

Perhaps Rousseau thought of these matters as he made his way to shore. Most likely, he was admiring the view. Ahead of him lay the town that Russians called New Archangel and Tlingit Indians referred to as Sitka. The peak known as Mount Verstovia towered over the town. Rousseau later wrote that it was a "bright and beautiful" day.[1]

Secretary of State Seward had dreamed of an elaborate transfer ceremony, with banquets, toasts, and speeches. Such events, however, were the last things on Rousseau's mind. He and Pestchouroff had been traveling since mid-August 1867. It was now October 18. Furthermore, the *John L. Stevens* had been waiting in the harbor for ten days. The ship's commander, who followed a diplomatic custom, would not allow its troops to go ashore until Rousseau's arrival. The diplomats had decided to have a quick ceremony and finish the transfer as soon as possible.

Rousseau reached the wharf and passed a battery of ancient guns. He saw several two-story warehouses, painted yellow with red sheet-iron roofs. Inside these warehouses were furs worth several hundreds of thousands of dollars.

Sitka hardly qualified as a world-class capital. A special correspondent who accompanied the troops commented, "Really, there is only one street in the town. . . . [It] terminates in the only road leading from town. It runs along the shore for a mile and turning north is stopped at the base of a jagged mountain."[2]

Even without roads, the town showed plenty of bustle on this October day. Families loaded with baggage walked along the streets. They were waiting for boats that would take them to Russia once the transfer was completed. Meanwhile, carpenters were busy making crates to hold pianos, books, and clothes for these emigrants. For most of the travelers, departure was a sad prospect. An American observer noted that the Russians "seemed as though they were preparing for the funeral of the Tsar [Russian emperor], going about the town in a most dejected manner."[3]

Others in town were considerably less unhappy. Businessmen from San Francisco had come here for the transfer. The Russian-American Company, which had governed the colony for more than sixty years, would soon be out of business. The company owned most of the property on Sitka and would have no further use for it. The businessmen hoped to obtain the company's surplus goods at low prices.

Rousseau met Jefferson C. Davis, who would become the acting governor of the new American territory. Pestchouroff met with Prince Maksutov, the outgoing Russian-American Company governor. They agreed to hold the transfer ceremony that afternoon.

More than two hundred people climbed a hill to the governor's residence for the transfer. Russian soldiers in their dark, red-trimmed uniforms showed up promptly at three o'clock. American troops soon joined them. Several businessmen came to watch the ceremony. Few of the Russian inhabitants bothered to attend the proceedings. For them, losing the colony they called home

SOURCE DOCUMENT

ART. I. . . . HIS MAJESTY THE EMPEROR OF ALL THE RUSSIAS AGREES TO CEDE TO THE UNITED STATES, BY THIS CONVENTION, IMMEDIATELY UPON THE EXCHANGE OF THE RATIFICATIONS THEREOF, ALL THE TERRITORY AND DOMINION NOW POSSESSED BY HIS SAID MAJESTY ON THE CONTINENT OF AMERICA AND IN THE ADJACENT ISLANDS. . . .

ART. III. . . . THE INHABITANTS OF THE CEDED TERRITORY, ACCORDING TO THEIR CHOICE, RESERVING THEIR NATURAL ALLEGIANCE, MAY RETURN TO RUSSIA WITHIN THREE YEARS; BUT, IF THEY SHOULD PREFER TO REMAIN IN THE CEDED TERRITORY, THEY, WITH THE EXCEPTION OF UNCIVILIZED NATIVE TRIBES, SHALL BE ADMITTED TO THE ENJOYMENT OF ALL THE RIGHTS, ADVANTAGES, AND IMMUNITIES OF CITIZENS OF THE UNITED STATES, AND SHALL BE MAINTAINED AND PROTECTED IN THE FREE ENJOYMENT OF THEIR LIBERTY, PROPERTY, AND RELIGION. . . . [4]

In the treaty for the purchase of Alaska, signed on March 30, 1867, Russia agreed to cede its former American colony to the United States.

was a sad occasion. Only a dozen women attended, including Princess Maksutova, the wife of the governor.

Several Tlingit chiefs showed up. In the past, members of the tribe had been bitter enemies of the Russians. Now they were honored guests. The Tlingit, however, were unhappy about the turn of events. Years before, they had sold land to the Russians. They had not expected the Russians to sell it to someone else. The Tlingit, however, realized they could do nothing to block the sale.

As three-thirty approached, the spectators waited around the ninety-foot-high flagpole. Soon Russia's Imperial Eagle flag would be taken down and the thirty-seven-star Old Glory raised. Pestchouroff gave the signal to lower the Russian flag and . . . it got stuck!

Rousseau later wrote to Secretary of State Seward:

> The ceremony was interrupted by the catching of the Russian flag in the ropes attached to the flag-staff. The soldier who was lowering it, continuing to pull at it, tore off the border by which it was attached, leaving the flag entwined tightly around the ropes. . . . [5]

After a while, a Russian soldier was lifted up and he threw down the uncooperative flag. It landed on a Russian soldier's bayonet. Princess Maksutova, already overwhelmed by the idea of having to leave her adoptive home, fainted.

The tangled flag marked an appropriate end to Russian America. The Western Hemisphere colony was supposed to be a peaceful and prosperous source of fur income. It had provided furs but little peace. In less than a century of Russian settlement, the colony had seen fights with natives; continuous disputes with Americans, British, and Spaniards; and even visits from a pirate ship of the defeated Confederate States of America.

Rousseau's private secretary raised the American flag. Then Russian and American soldiers alternated in firing salutes. Pestchouroff spoke a few words, turning over the land to the Americans, and Rousseau accepted it. This ended the transfer ceremony.

Rousseau felt sorry for the departing Russians. He wrote: "Three cheers were then spontaneously given

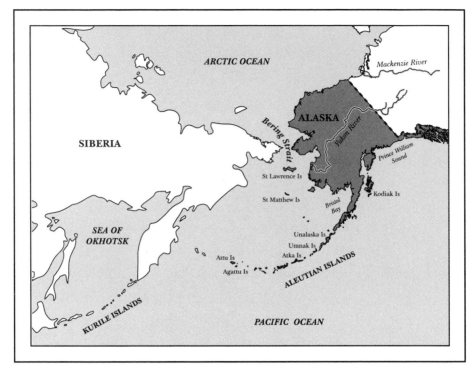

Russia ceded a huge amount of land, with very few European inhabitants, to the United States in 1867.

for the United States flag by the American citizens present, although this was not part of the programme, and on some accounts I regretted that it occurred."[6]

If Rousseau pitied the Russians, other Americans felt unrestrained joy. A California newspaper reporter wrote:

> The Russian eagle has now given place to the American, and the national colors flew over a new independent territory. Our dominion now borders on a new ocean and almost touches the old continent—Asia. . . . The occasion inspired the soul of every American present. . . . Three mighty cheers were given and we all rejoiced that we now stood on American soil.[7]

By 1740, European explorers had traveled to every inhabited part of the earth except for the northwestern coast of North America. Though unknown to Europeans, this region of North America was home to cultures that had flourished for thousands of years.

2

EARLY LIFE IN "THE GREAT LAND"

The First Alaskans

Throughout history, hunters have traveled in search of food. More than ten thousand years ago, that search took them across a treeless plain now known as Beringea.

Beringea no longer exists, at least not above water. During the last ice age, which ended about eleven thousand years ago, cold temperatures caused water to freeze, creating a land bridge between present-day Siberia and Alaska. Sea level dropped as much as three hundred feet, making a plain a thousand miles wide. Between twelve and twenty thousand years ago, early people crossed the frozen landscape. By about ten thousand years ago, the bridge was gone. Rising temperatures melted the glacial ice, separating present-day North America and Asia.

By then, the earliest North Americans had wandered all over the continent. Many stayed in its northern region. Archaeologists have found more than twenty-seven hundred sites in present-day Alaska. Trail Creeks Cove, north of Nome, contained a fifteen-thousand-year-old cracked bison skull. Ipiutak, the largest known prehistoric Alaska site, had six hundred partly underground homes.

The early men and women went to places with several different climates and landscapes. They adjusted to each, matching their food and clothing to the lands around them. By the time the first Europeans appeared, there were three major groups living along the Alaskan coast: Northwest Coast Indians, Eskimo, and Aleuts.

Northwest Coast Indians

Life was not harsh for the Tlingit and Haida, the Northwest Coast Indians. They lived in the area now known as the Panhandle, on Alaska's southeastern coast. The mild climate and plentiful game enabled them to develop one of the most advanced native cultures of the Americas.

Tlingit, Haida, and other tribes feasted on salmon, herring, and candlefish. Abundant sea mammals—sea otters, walruses, and whales—provided other food. Even though mountains prevented the tribes from going far inland, they sometimes hunted for bears, deer, and wolves. They apologized to nature for every animal life they took.

With so much food available, the Northwest Coast Indians had little need to worry about survival. They had leisure time. They used that time to produce some of the finest woodcrafts in the world. Finely carved and decorated canoes showed their artistic skill. So did the entrances to their homes. These artists showed amazing variety. "In the thousands upon thousands of Tlingit carvings, no two bowls or spoons or boxes or totem poles are exactly alike," noted art historian Leon Gordon Miller.[1]

Most notable were totem poles. Southeastern tribes, particularly the Haida, excelled in creating huge wooden poles with animal or human figures. These elaborate figures were called totems (emblems). They described the lives and the history of the families of the villages. "You treat a totem pole with respect, just like a person, because in our culture that's what it is," claimed totem pole carver Norman Tait. "A pole is just another person that is born into the family, except he is the storyteller. So it should be treated with respect and honor."[2]

The raising of a totem pole, or any

Distinctively carved totem poles served as family histories for the Tlingit and Haida Indians.

Russians never completely conquered the Tlingit, shown here dressed in tribal costumes.

other special occasion, called for a potlatch. Guests came from many miles away for these extravagant festivals. Hosts displayed their wealth by offering gifts and generous quantities of food to those guests.

The Tlingit were also particularly fearsome fighters. They occasionally lost battles. But no one, not even the Russians, succeeded in conquering them.

Eskimo

Most people think of frozen igloos made of blocks of ice when the word *Eskimo* is mentioned. Some of the *Inupiat* (Arctic Eskimo) lived in these dwellings. But

Eskimo thrived in a wide range of environments, from eastern Siberia east to Greenland, and from the Arctic Sea south to Kodiak Island, south of the Alaska mainland.

Some Eskimo lived in the interior, but most lived near the sea. They hunted whales and other sea mammals from *umiaks*, boats fifteen to forty feet long, or from smaller *kayaks*. They also hunted land animals. Eskimo used blankets to aid in their hunting. A hunter would move to the middle of a huge blanket. Villagers would then push the blanket upward so the hunter was tossed high into the air, where he could spot herds of distant animals.

Eskimo lived in villages of about two hundred people. Shamans were the most important village figures. These medicine men and women used dreams and visions to help solve the community's problems.

Aleuts

The bleak Aleutian Islands southwest of Alaska hardly seemed like a hospitable spot for people. "There are only two seasons: a long autumn and a short, mild winter," commented historian Vladimir Jochelson.[3] But those seasons could be devastating. Heavy rainfalls called *williwaws* pounded the windswept islands continuously. Most Aleuts considered themselves lucky if they saw seven to eight sunny days a year.

Aleuts adapted superbly to their treeless island setting. They built houses deep into the ground, covering them with driftwood or grass. These houses were constructed on the north sides of islands, where ocean currents were less troublesome.

Aleuts in their small boats (bidarkas) *were skilled hunters and fishermen.*

As oceangoing hunters, they had no equals. Aleuts paddled two-man waterproof boats, called *bidarkas*, in search of sea otters or seals. These boats carried hunters at great speed as they stalked their prey with bows and arrows, darts, spears, or harpoons. In their boats they could journey from island to island, or even to the mainland, which they called "Alyeska," or "the great land."[4]

Aleut culture and habits served them well against natural perils. But not even their many skills could protect them from the human invaders who would encounter them.

Never before had a people conquered so much land in so little time. In less than sixty years, Russia gained a landmass greater in size than the United States. A few thousand men, lacking charts, instruments, or knowledge of the land that lay ahead, expanded Russia's boundaries all the way from the Ural Mountains on the western edge of Asia to the Pacific Ocean.

IN SEARCH OF "SOFT GOLD"

An Honorable Pirate

Yermak Timofeyevich was a river pirate. He and his band of *Cossacks* (Russian frontiersmen) roamed up and down Russia's Volga River, plundering wherever they could. They went after whatever goods were available. But one commodity was more valuable than all others.

For centuries, Russia had valued animal furs. They were worth so much that they were known as "soft gold."[1] The sable, a small minklike creature, was particularly prized. At one time, the pelt of a single sable could buy its owner a fifty-acre farm. *Promyshlenniki*, fur hunters who were independent of governments or other rules, caught these four-legged treasure chests.

Timofeyevich was one of the more successful of the promyshlenniki.

Timofeyevich's exploits caught the attention of Russia's government. The czar, Ivan IV, wanted him arrested for his piracy. Timofeyevich enlisted the aid of the powerful Stroganov family. The czar ordered the Stroganovs to return him to Moscow for trial. The family refused to hand him over.

Instead, Timofeyevich recruited more than eight hundred followers and crossed the Ural Mountains to do battle with the Tatars who ruled the area. The one-time pirate exercised absolute control over his troops. Any follower who disobeyed him was tied up, put inside a weighted sack, and thrown into a river.

The war with the Tatars lasted less than two years. In 1579, Timofeyevich and his Cossacks captured the key city of Sibir. This victory opened up the road to the east, a region known as Siberia. Timofeyevich became known as the "Conqueror of Siberia."[2]

The victory also meant the capture of the city's furs—about one hundred thousand rubles' (Russian currency) worth. Timofeyevich did not keep the booty for himself. A folk song explained:

> *Dreaded Czar . . . accept respectful greetings from Yermak [Timofeyevich]*
>
> *As a gift I offer you the whole Siberian land.*
>
> *Yes, the whole Siberian land: grant a pardon to Yermak!*[3]

He turned the city and its furs over to the czar in exchange for freedom for himself and his men. He became a national hero. Timofeyevich died a few years later, but Russia held the gateway to Siberia and whatever lands lay beyond.

On to Siberia

With the fortress city of Sibir conquered, a parade of Russians moved into the Asian land. Fur traders and trappers came first, followed closely by Cossacks, government officials, and priests of the Russian Orthodox Church.

The Siberian road did not extend far into the 5-million-square-mile territory. Rivers provided the chief means of travel. Within twenty years of Timofeyevich's death, Russians had advanced to the Ob River in western Siberia. They pressed farther east to other mighty north-flowing rivers, the Yenesei and the Lena.

Russians opened up the Siberian frontier at a rate of about sixty miles per year. Often they had no clue about what lay ahead. They moved across rivers and swamps, past tundras (frozen plains), and through forests. In the summer they traveled on rafts, barges, and riverboats. During the winter they used sleds. Life was anything but easy. Russian author Sergei Nikoleivich Markov said the typical Siberian explorer "sleeps on snow, feeds himself any way he can, goes for years without seeing fresh bread, and often eats pine bark and 'any old foul thing.'"[4]

Greed, not love of exploration, drove the men forward. Siberian writer Valentin Rasputin commented, "They behaved as if this land were in imminent danger of falling to an enemy forever, and thus they had to take out everything that the enemy might be able to use."[5]

Wherever they traveled, the Russians built *ostrags* (forts), at about sixty-mile intervals. Although many Siberian natives gave up with little or no struggle, the forts assured that Russia would maintain military strength. Just as important, the forts served as trading centers. There the government collected the *yasak*, the fur tax demanded of the conquered natives. One notorious collector from the Siberian city of Yakutsk claimed he killed natives, burned their villages, and seized their property with "God's help."[6]

Once this system was established, other inhabitants followed. Some were criminals only a few steps ahead of the law in western Russia. Others were serfs who fled their former homes. Serfs were little better than slaves living on land owned by nobles. However, they were given all the land they could farm if they settled in Siberia. Russian nobles, without serfs to do physical labor for them, generally stayed away from Siberia.

In 1639 a small party led by Andrei Kapilof crossed the Stanovoi Mountains on the eastern edge of Siberia. They built a fort, Okhotsk, on the shore. Russia now had a foothold on the Pacific Ocean, fifty-eight hundred miles away from St. Petersburg.

Russians and Chinese

Even as the Russians moved eastward, they also looked elsewhere for trade. To the south lay the mysterious land of China, rumored to hold fabulous wealth. Russian traders wanted access to the silk, satin, cotton, and exotic foods of this huge land.

As early as 1616, Russians made serious attempts to open trade with China. Two years later, China's

The crest and coat of arms, at top, marked Russian nobility.

ruler, Altyn Khan, agreed to accept a trade party. The mission was not successful for the Russians. The Chinese declared they were not interested in trade and sent the Russians home.

In 1632, however, a Chinese agent told officials in the Siberian town of Tomsk that China was ready to discuss trade with the Russians. Altyn Khan agreed to be the middleman in dealings between merchants of the two countries.

Russia, meanwhile, moved into the fertile region of Manchuria in the 1640s. This area, along the eastward-flowing Amur River, grew crops and raised livestock of great value to the growing Siberian population. Manchus, however, fought back. In 1658, they drove the Russians from the Amur Valley. At about this time, Altyn Khan died. When he passed away, Chinese interest in Russian trade largely disappeared.

The Russians tried another Amur invasion in 1668. A former Polish prisoner of war named Nikefor Chernigovskii led the assault. By 1681, the Chinese Army had repelled the invaders. Russia lost even the right to navigate the Amur River. A treaty opened trade with China. But the major Asian food center was gone.

Peter the Great

Six thousand miles away from Peking (now Beijing), China, important activity was taking place in western Russia. A new, powerful man had assumed the throne as czar in 1689. Peter I, known as Peter the Great, was nearly seven feet tall. His actions would be even more impressive than his height. German philosopher Gottfried Leibniz declared, "the providence of God . . . has raised up such a furious man to so absolute authority over so great a part of the world."[7]

For centuries, western Europeans had viewed Russia as a backward, semicivilized land, more a home of Asian peasants than of European intellectuals. Peter tried to combat that image. He traveled through Europe, visiting England and the Netherlands. He gave women a greater role in society. He required noblemen to shave their beards, because clean-shaven faces were the Western style. He moved the capital from inland Moscow to the Baltic port of St. Petersburg because he felt he needed to "open a window" onto the sea and the West.[8] From the new capital, he built Russia's navy. Peter ordered secular (nonreligious) books published and even edited the country's first newspaper.

Science fascinated the energetic czar. He showed interest in the geography of the North Pacific region. Those unknown lands raised many questions. Were Asia and North America joined in the North Atlantic Ocean? Did a passage separate the two continents? Or was there an undiscovered continent in the middle of the ocean? What was out there?

4

"DISCOVER AMERICA"

Czar Peter I was not the only Russian who was curious about what lay beyond Siberia. In 1648 an explorer named Simeon Deshneff claimed that he had sailed around the East Cape, the northeasternmost part of Siberia, but he lacked adequate records to back up his report. In 1711 a Cossack named Popoff sailed around the cape. He mentioned a land called Alaska in his journal.

Peter the Great wanted more definite information. He sought a veteran, skilled leader to head an eastern expedition. Vitus Bering was that man.

An Administrator, Not an Adventurer

There are adventurers and there are administrators. Adventurers seek the thrill of discovering the unknown. Administrators preside over a group of workers. Vitus Bering was an administrator. The Danish native, born in 1681, moved to Russia at a young age and served more than twenty years in the Russian Navy. Czar Peter noticed Bering's fine work as director of military transportation during a war with Sweden in the early 1700s. After the war, Bering retired to Sweden. But the czar had one more task for him.

Peter called for an expedition to find a water route, if one existed, between Siberia and North America. It would be one of his last acts. Peter died in 1725, shortly after ordering the project. His widow and successor, Catherine I, continued approval of it.

Two groups totaling thirty-three explorers and seventy-two supply wagons left St. Petersburg in early 1725. They spent more than two years journeying through Siberia. During the summer, the parties used rafts and flatboats to travel along the great Siberian rivers. In wintertime, they hauled supplies over mountains on sleds through blinding snowstorms and subzero temperatures. At Yakutsk, they purchased six hundred horses for transportation. They reached Okhotsk in early fall and spent the winter of 1727–1728 there.

The following spring, they sailed to the Kamchatka peninsula. Because the southern part of the peninsula had not yet been explored, Bering had no idea how large it was. Taking no chances, he and his explorers crossed the peninsula by foot, then built a small boat named the *Saint Gabriel*.

"The Instructions . . . Had Been Carried Out"

Bering set sail on July 14, 1728, to "discover America."[1] His trip, although taking only seven weeks, would immortalize him.

In August, Bering spotted an island. He named it St. Lawrence Island, after the patron saint of the date, August 11. Four days later, the *Saint Gabriel* passed East Cape. Bering's boat moved between mainland Asia and North America at their closest point, less than fifty-five miles apart. Fog prevented him from viewing the North American mainland. Bering described the fog as "a mist so thick we could hardly see the length of our ship."[2]

Bering sailed to 67 degrees, 18 minutes north latitude. Then he turned around to go home. "The coast did not exist further north, and no other land was near," he explained in his journal.[3]

He believed there was land to the east, because he had seen driftwood and birds coming from that direction. Furthermore, natives had told him that a man stranded on an island had told them that he had come from the east. But Bering showed little inclination toward looking for this eastern land. "It seemed to me that the instructions of her Imperial Majesty had been carried out," he said after passing East Cape.[4] He and the crew spent the winter in Kamchatka, sailed around the peninsula to Okhotsk the following spring, and returned to St. Petersburg in 1730.

His journey met with less than total praise. When Bering addressed Russian senior officers and the Russian legislature, one commentator wrote: "Some clapped their hands while others shrugged their shoulders."[5] Imperial officials and the Royal Academy of Sciences complained about what they considered poor results.

"The Most Gigantic Geographic Enterprise"

Despite the supposed failure of the Bering voyage, the Russian Crown wanted another expedition. Czarina Anna, who became the ruler of Russia in 1730, wanted Bering to lead it.

If the first Bering journey was a major event, the second one would be an extravaganza. Historian Leonhard Stejneger called it "the most gigantic geographic enterprise undertaken by any government at any time."[6] More than nine hundred people would travel along all or part of the trip.

Czarina Anna presented an incredible list of expectations. She wanted Bering and his crew to discover and explore the North American continent, all the way to Mexico. She also wanted the party to explore and map all of Siberia; follow Siberian rivers to the Arctic Ocean and chart the northern coast; give detailed reports on plants, animals, and minerals along the way; study the language and folklore of the natives; and establish relations with Japan. If these tasks were not enough, the Bering expedition was also ordered to raise cattle on the Pacific coast, establish schools and a shipyard in Okhotsk, and build an iron works in Yakutsk. Many of these requests were time-consuming. Some, such as the complete map of Siberia, were downright impossible. And Bering was fifty-two years old, a ripe old age for an explorer. But he was willing to lead the expedition.

Among the expedition members were thirty scientists. Many expected life's luxuries and brought along cases of the finest wine. Often, they did little but get in Bering's way. He could not interfere with their activities, yet he was forced to bring them along. He needed patience and experience to handle this temperamental group.

Louis Delisle de la Croyere, an astronomer who wore waistcoats and lace cuffs, was one such scientist.

He brought nine wagons full of supplies with him. Bering also had to deal with naturalist Georg Steller, who wore smelly clothes and displayed an irritating, know-it-all attitude.[7]

The first expedition members left St. Petersburg in February 1733. Bering left with the last party to make sure the other travelers were proceeding well. The group spent the next five years trudging through Siberia. They had to bring all kinds of supplies along. Hundreds of workers and their families transported anchors, nails, tools, canvas, food, animals, medical supplies, and scientific equipment. They built two eighty-by-twenty-nine-foot boats, the *St. Peter* and *St. Paul*, in Okhotsk, then sailed to Kamchatka.

By the time the expedition had reached Kamchatka, its members had accomplished several of the assigned tasks. Various parties had navigated the rivers, studied Siberian life, and sailed to Japan. But the work was only beginning. The Bering crew built Petropavlovsk, a settlement on the Pacific coast of Kamchatka, then prepared for a long eastward journey. Bering, meanwhile, had to deal with eccentric scientists, surly crew members, and pompous town officials all the way through Asia. By the time the ships were ready to sail in June 1741, Vitus Bering was a tired man.

"This . . . Must Be America"

From the start, the journey appeared to be a mistake. De la Croyere mistakenly believed that a huge island lay to the southeast of Kamchatka. Bering in the *St. Peter* and Imperial Navy officer Alexei Chirikov in the *St. Paul* started off looking for that nonexistent island.

The two officers planned to keep their ships together. But early in the voyage, a storm separated them. Bering and Chirikov never saw each other again.

Chirikov spotted land first. On July 15, 1741, he saw an island off Alaska's southeast coast. *St. Paul* crew members saw "some very high mountains, their summits covered in snow, their lower slopes, we thought, covered in trees. This, we thought, must be America."[8]

The commander sent a boat ashore to explore the newly discovered land. The ten-member boat did not return. He dispatched a seven-man boat to search for the first one. It did not return either. Later, two boats approached the *St. Paul*. Natives in the boats shouted something at the Russians and returned to land. Chirikov never saw another trace of the boats or the men. A legend of the Tlingit Indians claims that warriors dressed in bear skins led them to an ambush and killed them.

More than men were lost. The *St. Paul* had lost both of its lifeboats. That meant that ship members could not go ashore to collect freshwater. By the end of September, only nine of forty-five barrels had water. That number dropped to six two weeks later.

Without the help of friendly natives, that number would have been even less. The *St. Paul* encountered some natives greeting the ship from an Aleutian island. Chirikov somehow got the message across to them that his crew needed water. The natives supplied the precious fluid, and Chirikov continued to Kamchatka.

Even the water could not prevent an attack of scurvy. The ship lacked the fresh fruits and vegetables that provided vitamin C, which would fight the disease.

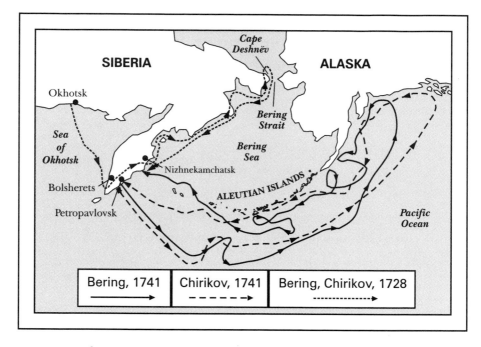

SIBERIA

Cape
Deshnëv

ALASKA

Okhotsk

Bering
Strait

Sea
of
Okhotsk

Bering
Sea

Nizhnekamchatsk

Bolsherets

ALEUTIAN ISLANDS

Petropavlovsk

Pacific
Ocean

| Bering, 1741 | Chirikov, 1741 | Bering, Chirikov, 1728 |

Explorers Vitus Bering and Alexei Chirikov passed the Bering Strait on Bering's 1728 voyage. In 1741, Bering and Chirikov's ships separated. Both perished before they could return to Siberia.

Chirikov lost twenty men to scurvy. The commander himself was flattened by it. Chirikov wrote: "Many members of the crew are seriously ill, due to a lack of water and the long and arduous voyage. More than half the crew are unable to work."[9] They barely made it back to Kamchatka. The ship had only one barrel of freshwater left.

" . . . What Accidents May Yet Happen"

Bering, meanwhile, had sailed hundreds of miles away from the companion ship. On July 16, 1741, the *St.*

Peter found land later known as Kayak Island. The sun broke through rain clouds, presenting a beautiful view of a snow-capped mountain towering over a forested island. The members of the expedition named the peak Mount St. Elias. They had discovered America from the Pacific Ocean.

Steller wrote that Bering failed to share his crew's enthusiasm: "Nobody failed to congratulate the Captain Commander. . . . He, however, received it all not only very indifferently and without particular pleasure, but in the presence of all he even shrugged his shoulders while looking at the land."[10]

Bering had other concerns, mainly the safety of his men and adequate supplies to return home. Steller recorded Bering as saying, "Now we think that we have found everything and many are full of expectations like pregnant windbags. But they do not consider where we have reached land, how far we are from home, and what accidents may yet happen."[11]

However, Bering permitted the crew to go ashore and get freshwater. Steller, after considerable pleading, was allowed to accompany them. Even so, their stay on the island lasted only a short time. "Ten years getting to America, and a miserable ten hours ashore," the naturalist grumbled.[12]

Bering's worries were not groundless. Scurvy attacked the crew of the *St. Peter* in August. By September, it had become an epidemic. The crew had little choice but to return to Kamchatka. First mate Sven Waxel wrote: "When it came to a man's turn at the helm, he was dragged to it by two other of the invalids who were still able to walk a little. . . . When he could sit no more, he had to be replaced by another in no better case than he."[13]

In early November, Bering sighted land he believed to be the Siberian peninsula. Fierce winds and waves drove the ship into rocks offshore. Water entered the remains of the ship, destroying its bread supply.

By now, twelve of the crew had already died of scurvy, thirty-four were totally disabled, and ten others could move only with difficulty. The few healthy crew members moved their companions, including Bering, to shore. For several, the captain included, the move stalled death only briefly. Within a month, Vitus Bering was gone. He died on the Bering Strait island that now bears his name.

Crew members who were able dug sand dwellings and gathered food for their mates. Slowly, many of the others' health improved. They caught and ate sea otters and sea cows, animals unknown in Russia. They made otter skins into warm, waterproof clothing. By the spring of 1742, the crew was ready to attempt a trip home.

In May 1742, Chirikov went looking for the *St. Peter*. He passed the island where Bering's crew was stranded but did not see them. Then he sailed back to Kamchatka. He returned to St. Petersburg in 1746.

Sven Waxel and his crew built a new ship from the remains of the *St. Peter*. They left the island in mid-August and returned to Petropavlovsk two weeks later. The cramped boat did not even have room for men to lie down. But the crew did not come back empty-handed. They carried a fortune in furs, enough to make the voyage profitable.

"The Pioneer of Alaskan Natural History"

Furs brought material wealth to the Russian Empire. But for scientific knowledge, and perhaps the *St. Peter*'s crew's lives, Russians had to thank Georg Steller.

German-born Steller had gone to Russia in 1734 and approached the Royal Academy of Sciences. He applied for and received a job with Bering's expedition. For much of the trip, other members, including Bering and Waxel, would have little to do with him.

During the trip, Steller had begged to go to Kayak Island, and Bering finally agreed. In his few hours on shore, Steller was a whirlwind of activity. He collected more than a hundred plant species, plus birds, fish, and mammals. He discovered a hollowed log filled with water and recently heated stones. Nearby he discovered reindeer antlers, sheep bones, and dried fish—a sign that nearby natives had just cooked a meal. Steller's

SOURCE DOCUMENT

EVERY MOMENT WE EXPECTED THE DESTRUCTION OF OUR VESSEL, AND NO ONE COULD LIE DOWN, SIT UP, OR STAND. NOBODY WAS ABLE TO REMAIN AT HIS POST: WE WERE DRIFTING UNDER THE MIGHT OF GOD WHITHER THE ANGRY HEAVENS WILLED TO SEND US. HALF OF OUR CREW LAY SICK AND WEAK, THE OTHER HALF WERE OF NECESSITY ABLE-BODIED BUT QUITE CRAZED AND MADDENED FROM THE TERRIFYING MOTION OF THE SEA AND SHIP.[14]

Georg Steller's journal from October 1741 detailed the perilous journey he and his fellow explorers had undertaken in the exploration of Alaska.

suspicions were confirmed years later. An aging Eskimo told a trader that as a boy, he had seen white men who fit the description of the Bering expedition.

The naturalist made a phenomenal discovery—a jay. The bird resembled a picture he had seen in an English book about birds of the Carolinas. "This bird proved to me that we were really in America," Steller wrote.[15]

He also described animals unknown in Russia, such as the sea otter, sea lion, and fur seal. Most amazing was a gigantic marine mammal unlike anything that Russians had seen before, now called Steller's sea cow. These sea cows were thirty to forty feet long, ten to twelve feet thick. When hunters killed one in June 1742, it took forty men to drag it to shore. Steller dissected the animal and made detailed descriptions of its appearance and structure. If not for his writing, little would be known of this North Pacific beast. Within a generation, Russian hunters would lead to its extinction.

Steller had learned from natives that certain plants cured scurvy. When reluctant shipmates agreed to try his medicine, their conditions improved. Steller died while returning to St. Petersburg, but his book *De Bestiis Marinis* was published later. Biographer Leonhard Stejneger has called Steller "the pioneer of Alaskan natural history."[16]

They were frisky creatures about five feet long and two feet wide, with fur three quarters of an inch thick. Sea otters abounded on North Pacific islands in the 1740s. Within two generations, they faced extinction.

EXPLOITATION, NOT PARTNERSHIP

Never had an animal become more commercially valuable. Sea otter pelts meant warmth and beauty to people throughout Europe and China. Promyshlenniki made fortunes from the sea otters and other fur-bearing mammals. These fortunes came at the cost of the lives of hundreds of thousands of animals and even thousands of humans.

A Compass, a Sextant, Charts, and Wits

A more unlikely group of sea explorers might be hard to imagine. Most Russian promyshlenniki were not seagoers. They knew foot power or horsepower, not wind power. Most carried only a compass, a sextant (an instrument used to determine latitude), very primitive charts, and their wits. They knew little beyond islands they had already visited. If a ship lost its course, the crew often fired the ship's navigator on the spot and prayed for help. Yet these traders and trappers

Fur seals (above) and sea otters abounded in North Pacific islands. Russians used their furs as the basis of Russian America's economy.

were the leading figures in Russia's early ventures into North America.

Promyshlenniki had largely depleted the Siberian fur supply by the 1740s. But news of sea otters and other four-legged and flippered treasures spurred them to unimaginable Pacific dreams. They heard stories of millions of fur seals on the Pribilof Islands, whose barking was so loud that it sounded like a continuous thunderstorm. Sea lions and sea cows rested by the thousands on coastal rocks, waiting to be hunted.

Experienced seamen stayed away from such foolish ventures. An estimated one third of the traders who set out for furs never came back. But if the risks were great, so were the profits.

Often, these profits came at the hands of natives. Historian W. H. Pierce wrote:

> The prices received by the natives were very low. For example, traders would exchange an old fashioned flint lock shotgun for furs. . . . They would hold the gun upright on the floor, and the Indian who bought it had to pay for it [with] a pile of . . . skins up to the top of the gun. Every skin would be worth five or six dollars in the home market. Thus they realized five or six hundred dollars for an article not worth ten.[1]

Emilian Basov was one of the first of these adventurers. Financed by a Siberian trader named Andrei Serebrenikov, he spent the winter of 1743 at Bering Island. His catch proved so successful that he went back for a second winter. Basov's crew brought back sixteen hundred sea otter pelts, two thousand fur seals, and two thousand blue fox. The pelts earned him about two hundred thousand rubles for the winter's work.

With that amount of money available, it was little wonder that trappers would go out hunting for three to five years at a time. It was less wonder that Siberian financiers were willing to back these voyagers, in exchange for 40 percent of the profits. Between 1750 and 1775, six to twelve ships left Kamchatka every year, seeking furry fortunes.

" . . . Derive the Greatest Benefit From Them"

On September 25, 1745, a promyshlenniki ship landed on Attu. Crew members explored and exploited this westernmost of the Aleutian Islands. Promyshlenniki made no attempts to save some animals so they could breed in the future. When the hunters depleted the resources of one island, they traveled farther and farther away from Siberia. In months and years to come, trappers would use Atka, Adak, Unimak, Unalaska, and other Aleutian Islands as stepping-stones to furs and profits.

From the beginning, relations with the Aleuts went badly. A trader named Yakov Chuprov landed at Agattu Island. An observer noted,

> Several inhabitants appeared on the coast and the pilot was making towards shore in the small boat, with an intention to landing. . . . He contented himself therefore with flinging some needles amongst them: the islanders in return threw into the boat some sea-fowl. . . .[2]

Chuprov, however, reportedly soon tired of the trade. The Aleuts wished to continue bartering and wanted one of the Russians' muskets. Chuprov refused such a deal. Accidentally or not, a gun went off, wounding an Aleut in the arm.

Chuprov wintered on the Aleutian Islands. He and his men adopted the Aleuts' diet of fish, sea mammals, shellfish, eggs, and berries. Like the Aleuts, they used animal furs for clothing. They employed the Aleuts to hunt furs for them, but did not always pay the natives for their efforts.

A trader named Adriian Tolstykh proved kinder to the natives. He greeted the local chief with respect and gave him a copper bottle and Russian clothing. His kindness helped land the ship five hundred thousand rubles worth of furs, thanks to the natives' help.

Cruelty, rather than kindness, was the rule, however. Russian traders often killed Aleut men and raped Aleut women. One such slaughter at Attu Harbor gave it the name Massacre Bay.

The traders exacted *yasak* (tribute) from natives. Czarina Elizabeth, who came to power in 1741, ordered a royal collector to go with every vessel, to assure that the government collected this native tax. Natives, quite rightly, resented the yasak. What benefit would they get out of it? Would the czarina, seven thousand miles away, protect them? Still, they had little choice. The Aleuts learned early that their spears and bows and arrows were no match for the Russians' guns.

In 1762, a secret confederation of Aleuts throughout the islands planned a revolt. It caught the Russians by surprise. The Aleuts destroyed four of five ships located at Fox Island, killing most of the men aboard.

The Russians wasted little time in getting even. Their revenge was ruthless. They slaughtered thousands of the natives, often in a savage manner. One navigator, Ivan Soloviev, lined up a dozen Aleuts in single file to see how many could be killed by one bullet. The bullet killed nine of them.

A different revolt took place that year in St. Petersburg. Nobles ousted Czar Peter III and replaced him with his wife. Catherine II, known as Catherine the Great, would rule for more than thirty years as one of Russia's most effective monarchs.

Catherine had more interest in European affairs than in eastern happenings. But she did not ignore the American territory. Catherine called for an expedition "for the purpose of obtaining a description of some hitherto unknown islands, in order that it may be possible to derive the greatest benefit from them."[3]

That mission came back with a recommendation: do away with the yasak. It reported that natives never understood the concept of taxes. Furthermore, the cost of collecting the tribute was almost equal to the revenue received. Catherine followed that suggestion.

Russians came to another realization after 1762. Aleutian men were worth more alive than dead. The Aleuts had told the Russians, "We live like our brother, the sea otter."[4] The natives lived among the animals and understood their moves. The Russians' clumsy attempts at hunting from boats were no match for the skills Aleuts had practiced since birth.

This did not mean that Russian hunters treated the Aleuts well. Catherine wanted to "impress upon the hunters the necessity of treating their new brethren and countrymen, the inhabitants of our newly-acquired islands, with greatest kindness."[5] Still, relations with the Aleuts became exploitation, not partnership.

The Aleut population numbered about twenty-five thousand at the time of the Russians' arrival. Contact with the traders and trappers took its toll. Aleuts died because of murder, bad treatment, and disease. Some died from starvation because their food supply—the sea animals they were hunting for their Russian masters—was becoming scarce. Within fifty years, 60 to 70 percent of the Aleut population was lost.

Spanish, French, and British Explorations

News of the abundant fur supply in the North Pacific could not stay hidden forever. Other countries began making their own voyages there, to investigate the wealth or secure land claims. Spain had appeared content with its colony along the coast of Mexico. There appeared to be no hurry to move northward. No other European power had settled along the North Pacific coast of North America. Besides, Spain had a centuries-old claim to all the land in the western part of the New World even if most other nations did not honor that claim.

Russian exploration of the North Pacific changed matters. Suddenly, the Spaniards found the need to take action. They built a series of missions and towns in California: San Diego in 1769, Monterey in 1770, San Francisco in 1776.

Beginning in 1773, the viceroy (colonial governor) of Mexico, ordered several explorations of the northwest coast. One, led by Lieutenant Francisco Quadro, went to 57 degrees north latitude, near present-day Sitka. Quadro claimed the area in the name of the queen of Spain. Spaniards also went farther north; they gave names to the present-day areas of Valdez and Cordova. Yet they made no attempts at permanent settlements.

France sent an explorer, Jean-François de Galaup de la Pérouse, to the Pacific coast in 1785. He sighted land near Mount St. Elias but did not send a landing party ashore. The Frenchman crossed the Pacific to Petropavlovsk, on the eastern side of the Kamchatka peninsula. There, he had his journals sent overland to Paris. He disappeared soon afterward. The wreckage of his ship was found later.

England sent its most honored explorer to the northern Pacific region. On two previous voyages, Captain James Cook had discovered previously unknown treasures in the ocean. His charts were so precise that even Russian traders used them.

On his first trip in 1768, he discovered Tahiti and mapped New Zealand and the eastern coast of Australia. On his second trip, he looked for a rumored southern continent. Cook's ships, the *Resolution* and *Discovery*, were the first to cross the Antarctic Circle, but packs of ice prevented him from visiting the continent of Antarctica.

His third voyage was the most significant of all. Cook discovered the Sandwich (now Hawaiian) Islands, then sailed north. He was looking for the rumored Northwest Passage, an ocean shortcut between the Pacific Ocean and northeast Canada's Hudson Bay, across the continent of North America. Cook also had received orders to take possession of all uninhabited

territories that he encountered even if European explorers had already visited there. He set up markers and left bottles with British coins and the name of his ship along his route.

English explorer James Cook traveled throughout the Pacific Ocean in the late 1700s, reaching as far north as Alaska.

Cook sailed along the Alaska coast, into the inlet that now bears his name. Thinking he had found a shortcut to the east, he sailed to the end of the inlet. He was forced to turn back at an area he called the Turnagain Arm. Cook sailed through the Bering Strait until ice blocked his path in August 1778. He returned to the Sandwich Islands for the winter but was slain by natives there in 1779.

Cook's ships never found the Northwest Passage (which does not exist), but his men found furs. When they sold their catch at Canton, China, for ten thousand dollars, they wanted to return for more. In years to come, British and American ships would become greatly involved in the fur trade.

Cook sailed up Cook Inlet (as it is now called), hoping in vain to find a shortcut across the North American continent.

The Need to Colonize

Cook's crew encountered some Russians near the Cook Inlet. The men from the two nations spent a few days together and apparently enjoyed the meeting. The Russian commander, however, did not share the enthusiasm. Russia had had the area and its furs to itself. The Russians did not welcome possible competition. But until the 1780s, Russia had done little to make a claim to the New World. There were no houses or warehouses. The rule of force was the only law. Russia's government had done little with the colonies except collect taxes from natives. Other countries had brought along religious officials to spread the Christian word to natives. The Russians had not done so.

By this time, the nature of fur trade was changing. Small ships no longer found the trade profitable. Larger ships owned by Siberian merchants now dominated the scene. These newer, larger, more modern ships would stay out for seven years at a time. Their captains sought ports for trade and protection.

Even these ships would have a hard time competing if the area could not be made safe. This could not be assured unless the area had Russian settlers. Someone, somehow, would have to build and maintain a colony on northwestern North American soil.

Grigory Ivanovich Shelekhov arrived in Siberia sometime in the 1760s. By the 1770s, he had staked out quite a reputation for himself. He was a great organizer, a shrewd businessman, and more than a bit of a liar.

THE AGE OF BARANOV

Ivan Golikov, another man with a colorful history, most likely knew of Shelekhov's reputation. Golikov had been exiled to Siberia several years earlier on embezzlement charges.

Together, the two men worked wonders. Merchant Shelekhov and financier Golikov started an enormously profitable company and led to the settlement of Russian America.

"The Russian Columbus"

Shelekhov knew that Russia's hold on the American territory was a weak one. Fur traders and trappers had put up temporary dwellings. But in forty years there, Russian America had no permanent European settlements. Furthermore, the Russian government was doing nothing to establish a colony there.

Since the government was not acting, Shelekhov decided to do something. He asked Golikov for money and went fifty thousand rubles into debt himself. He realized that such a project called for at least five years' worth of supplies. He would need at least three ships to carry food, seeds, livestock, firearms, tools, and most important, men.

By 1783, Shelekhov had rounded up the necessary men and materials. His three ships set sail in August containing two hundred men and one woman— Shelekhov's wife, Natalia.

Disaster struck almost immediately. They ran into a storm off the Kuril Islands. The *St. Michael*—the ship carrying the expedition's tools—was lost. The other ships spent the winter at Bering Island, hoping that their fellow ship would find them. There was no sign, however, and in the spring of 1784, both remaining ships sailed eastward.

They sighted Kodiak Island in July. Shelekhov found a stretch of grassy coast and landed there. He called the site Three Saints Bay, after the name of his lead ship. Shelekhov fended off an early attack attempt from the local Eskimo. "The savages came down from their rocks in great numbers, and fell upon us with such fury, that I verily believe they would have effected their purpose without difficulty, had we been less vigilant, or more timid," he later claimed.[1] However, once he defeated the Eskimo, he then sought to establish good relations with them.

Meanwhile, Shelekhov began building a colony. Bunkhouses, barns, storage buildings, a blacksmith's shop, and a carpentry shop soon appeared. Within a few months, the Russians had created several outposts on other islands. Shelekhov's energies on Kodiak and

G. I. Shelekhov, a fast-talking trader, became the founder of Russian America.

surrounding islands earned him the title the "Russian Columbus."[2]

By 1788, Shelekhov felt confident enough in the colony to return to Siberia. His work was far from over. Now he would go to Catherine the Great, seeking the money and supplies needed to enlarge the Russian-American holdings. First, he stopped at the eastern

Siberian city of Irkutsk. He flattered the governor, Ivan Yakolii, into giving him a good reference to give to the czarina.

Shelekhov, through Golikov, showed Catherine maps and papers from the colony. He also presented her with a lengthy wish list. Shelekhov sought a free government ship, clergy, farmers, skilled workers, military personnel, rights to establish a private port on the Sea of Okhotsk, and permission to trade with other Pacific nations. He also requested five hundred thousand rubles in a long-term loan, which amounted to a gift. Most important, he sought for his company a monopoly on trade in Russian America.

Catherine, at first, did not refuse these incredible demands outright. Instead, she requested that Shelekhov and Golikov meet her in St. Petersburg. She was impressed that they, without government help, had set up the colony.

Both arrived in the capital in early 1788. The two businessmen waited months for an audience with the monarch. Meanwhile, Catherine had changed her mind about aiding the colony. Russia was now at war with Sweden. Catherine believed that a Russian colony in the Pacific might anger the British, and she might need British help against the Swedes. Shelekhov and Golikov, therefore, received only swords and gold medals—a reward so trifling as to be considered an insult.

Shelekhov returned to Irkutsk. He wrote a self-serving, truth-bending book called *The Voyage of Grigory Shelekhov, Russian Merchant* while Golikov tried negotiating from the capital. In 1792, they received a break.

A lover of Catherine's used his influence with her for the company's benefit. She agreed to his request to provide clergy and farmers and buy thirty serfs. Shelekhov had promised to civilize the natives and bring religion to them. Catherine sent along a government official to make sure that Shelekhov kept those promises.

The last thing that Grigory Shelekhov wanted was a government busybody enforcing promises he had little intention of keeping. The government man, however, turned out to be a valuable ally. Nikolay Petrovich Rezanov, the young Russian nobleman, even married Shelekhov's daughter. Soon after the 1795 wedding, Shelekhov died and Golikov retired. But they left the Russian-American Company in good shape. Shelekhov's widow, Natalia, and son-in-law, Rezanov, were good managers. The most notable manager of all led the Russian-American colony.

"Somewhat of a Soldier, Somewhat of a Trader"

When Grigory Shelekhov left Russian America to return to Russia, he put merchant Ivan Soloviev in charge. He asked Soloviev to extend the colony as far south as California, keep out foreign traders, establish schools, build forts, and identify plant and animal life. Shelekhov wrote those instructions mainly to impress Catherine. He questioned Soloviev's qualifications to head the colony.

Shelekhov already had a replacement in mind. Aleksandr Baranov seemed to be the last person capable of governing a land larger than most European empires. But in nearly thirty years, he became the most notable person in Russian-American history.

Little hinted at greatness when he assumed charge of Russian America in 1790. The short, blond, balding man had little formal education. He lacked the social connections that were often necessary in that time. He had little business success in the past. He had worked as a store clerk in Moscow, then moved to Siberia. At first, he had refused Shelekhov's offer to direct Russian-American operations. Baranov's business failure in Siberia forced him to reconsider the offer.

He got off to a bad start. On his way to Kodiak Island, Baranov was shipwrecked near Unalaska Island. He spent the winter of 1790 there. In May 1791, he and sixteen shipmates sailed the last four hundred miles in an open boat. He came down with pneumonia, became delirious from the disease, and had to be carried ashore at Three Saints Bay.

That run-down village hardly lifted his spirits. The only settler who impressed him was a wooden-legged clerk named Ivan Kuskof. Baranov worked hard to earn the men's confidence. They feared him at first, and then finally came to admire him. He was "a rough, rugged, hospitable, hard-drinking, old Russian; somewhat of a soldier, somewhat of a trader; above all, a boon companion," wrote American author Washington Irving.[3]

Baranov's fortune tumbled in 1794, when the serfs, farmers, and clergymen requested by Shelekhov arrived. Baranov and the priests mistrusted each other from the start. The priests asked the company governor where the Three Saints church was. Baranov, unaware that Shelekhov had lied to them, asked, "What church?"[4] The priests disliked Baranov because he had left a wife and child in Russia and married a native chief's daughter. Most of all, they despised the governor because he made them do physical work like everyone else in the colony. Archimandrite Ioasaph, leader of the newly arrived priests, commented, "If I had to describe in detail all Baranov's evil acts I would have to write a book not a letter."[5]

However, Baranov's relations with the natives were good. He made an effort to learn native languages and customs. He listened to their problems and dealt with them fairly. Baranov hired natives as guides and made sure they were paid.

Baranov largely did whatever he pleased. "God is in Heaven and St. Petersburg is a long way off," he claimed.[6] He established a trading post at Cook Inlet. When a rival trading company set up a fort, he arrested the company's leader, even though he had no legal authority to do so. His methods did not bother his company superiors. Historian Frank A. Golder commented, "Baranov . . . worked for a company that demanded dividends and asked no questions as to means employed."[7]

The Russian-American Company

Colonial trading companies spread around the globe in the late 1700s. The Dutch East India Company traded tea and other goods in southeast Asian islands. The British East India Company likewise traded in India and surrounding areas. In North America, the

British-chartered Hudson's Bay Company set up trading posts in the Canadian territories.

To European governments, these companies provided several advantages. They explored Asian or American regions and set up colonies there. They provided revenue for the government back home. If the company did something the government approved, the government could take credit. If something went wrong, the government could deny responsibility. If the company developed a colony sufficiently well, the government could take it over.

Shelekhov and Golikov in 1783 had proposed to Catherine such a trading company to "sail to the land of Alaiksa [sic], which is called America, to islands known and unknown, in order to trade in furs, to make explorations and to arrange voluntary trade with the natives."[8] Later, Rezanov had recommended that all existing trading companies be united under his Russian-American Company.

Catherine had issued a *ukase* (decree) allowing the company control of regions already occupied by its agents. However, she did not issue the trade monopoly the company desired. Catherine died in 1796, and her son Paul I became czar. Paul signed a charter for the Russian-American Company in 1799. It gave the company exclusive trading rights in Russia's North American colonies for twenty years. One third of this new monopoly's profits would go to the Shelekhov family, one third would go to the Russian government, and one third to the merchants from rival companies who were forced to leave North America. Baranov, until then the manager of the company's

Russian-American holdings, became governor of the colony.

Life was no paradise for company workers in Alaska. Workers "are extremely ill-treated and kept at their work till their strength is entirely exhausted," claimed visiting German naturalist Georg Henry Langsdorff.[9] They lacked proper food and medical care. They could buy goods only at expensive company stores. As a result, most ended up in debt by the end of their seven-year terms with the company. Those owing money could be retained by the company until their debts were repaid. As a result, a seven-year term could end up as a lifetime job. Many, however, stayed voluntarily. They had married native women and raised families.

SOURCE DOCUMENT

THE COMPANY WAS GRANTED "THE PRIVILEGE OF CARRYING ON TO THE EXCLUSION OF OTHER RUSSIANS AND OF SUBJECTS OF FOREIGN STATES ALL INDUSTRIES CONNECTED WITH THE CAPTURE OF WILD ANIMALS AND ALL FISHING INDUSTRIES ON THE SHORE OF NORTHWESTERN AMERICA WHICH HAVE FROM TIME IMMEMORIAL BELONGED TO RUSSIA, COMMENCING FROM THE NORTHERN PART OF THE ISLAND OF VANCOUVER, UNDER 56° NORTH LATITUDE TO THE BERING STRAITS AND BEYOND THEM, AND ON THE ISLANDS WHICH BELONG TO THAT COAST. . . ."[10]

The Russian-American Company's charter gave it many rights and privileges.

The company wielded total control over Russians and natives alike. Natives had the right to complain about company policies, but the complaint had to be made to the company headquarters in St. Petersburg. Even the most powerful native chief lacked the time, energy, and money to spend thousands of rubles, travel thousands of miles, and waste thousands of days on a protest. Rather than fighting, most natives cooperated with the company.

New Archangel

Aleksandr Baranov was ambitious. He had strengthened the Russian colony at Kodiak Island. Now he looked to expand to the southeast. Baranov had visited the area the Tlingit called Sitka in 1793. He saw the Indians' tall totem poles and long communal houses. Baranov had a particular interest in the area and planned to build a colony there. Americans, who had recently gained independence from Great Britain, and the British had been trading there. Baranov was concerned that they were dealing weapons to the Indians.

On the way to Sitka, Baranov and his men had camped on a beach. Without warning, a Tlingit war party attacked them. Crew member Cyril Chlielinifof wrote:

> The Tlingits' armor . . . consisted of wooden rods bound together with leather thongs. Their faces were protected with masks which represented the heads of bears, dogfish, and other animals. . . . Their weapons consisted of lances, bows, and two pointed daggers. The Russians aimed directly at their heads, but the bullets did not penetrate the thick head covering.[11]

Baranov recalled, "What saved us from total destruction was the darkness, which prevented our assailants from distinguishing friend from foe."[12]

Six years later, he returned. More than one thousand settlers—most of them Aleuts in bidarkas—accompanied him on the six-hundred-mile journey. He tried to talk Tlingit Chief Skayeuletit into moving out of his village so that the Russians could set up a post there. Baranov finally built a settlement a few miles north of the Tlingit community.

Baranov had received instructions from company headquarters in St. Petersburg. "Don't make the places small. Have public squares, wide streets. Leave trees along the streets and in the yards. Place the houses well apart so that the town looks bigger."[13]

Such a picturesque town might have been good in theory, but Baranov did not trust the Tlingit. He built Fort St. Michael and a compact settlement next to it.

At first, the settlement proceeded peacefully. Foreign ships began arriving to trade in 1800. Thanks to a constant guard kept by Aleuts and Russians, the Tlingit refrained from attacks. By 1802, Baranov felt confident that the settlement could survive. He returned to Kodiak Island.

Shortly after Baranov left, disaster struck. Most of the men were out hunting, and those remaining had let down their guard. Suddenly a swarm of heavily painted Tlingit warriors scaled the fort's walls. They killed more than four hundred men and carried off women and children as prisoners.

Some Russian men survived the onslaught. They hid for eight days in a nearby forest. Captain Henry

Barber of the English ship *Unicorn* rescued them. Afterward, he invited the Tlingit chief and his nephew onto his ship. When they boarded, he put the Indians in irons. He threatened to kill them if the tribe did not hand over the hostages and furs that had been taken. Once he received the hostages and furs, Barber took them to Kodiak Island. He sought fifty thousand dollars from Baranov for the hostages but settled for ten thousand.

Baranov vowed revenge when he heard of the attack. He assembled a crew of "drunkards, adventurers, bankrupt traders and mechanics, or branded criminals in search of fortune" to recapture the fort.[14] Two sloops, two schooners, and 300 bidarkas carried 168 promyshlenniki and 500 Aleuts to Sitka. Soon a powerful reinforcement joined them. The *Neva*, a Russian frigate that had arrived at Kodiak Island shortly after Baranov had left, followed and caught up with the governor's fleet.

The Tlingit, upon seeing the *Neva*, agreed to talk with Baranov. Chief Katlian was stalling for time. He hoped for reinforcements from neighboring tribes, which never came. The Aleuts, meanwhile, towed the *Neva* into firing position in case the talks broke down.

Baranov told the Tlingit that they had to leave their island. The tribe refused, and Baranov returned to his ship. On September 26, 1804, the *Neva* began shelling the Tlingit fortress. Still the tribe would not yield. An assault unit rowed toward shore. The Tlingit fired back, killing ten men. Twenty-six others, including Baranov, were wounded. Yuri Lisianski, aboard the *Neva*, saw an Indian canoe with reinforcements and gunpowder. A perfectly aimed cannonball blew the canoe to pieces.

The bombardment continued for ten days. During the day, the Tlingit fired at the Russian and Aleut craft. At night, the chants of their medicine men kept the attackers awake all night. Then one night, the noise stopped. The Tlingit, out of ammunition, had crept out of their fort. The next day, scouts found more than thirty bodies. Five of those belonged to children. The Tlingit had killed the young ones rather than have noisy children alert their enemies of their escape.

Baranov wasted no time taking over the Tlingit site. He built a settlement there on a high, flat hill and named it New Archangel after a Russian seaport. It became the colony's capital. It was also North America's most important Pacific coast seaport. It had a cathedral, colleges, and the only shipyard north of Hawaii. New Archangel boasted a thousand people in the early 1800s, when Spanish-ruled San Francisco could claim only a few hundred.

Soon it became more than a fur trade center. New Archangel craftsmen made church bells for California missions, bricks for Russian fireplaces, and farm tools for as far away as Mexico. Tanneries, woolen manufacturers, and woodworking businesses appeared. A huge beacon greeted sailors at the harbor's entrance.

Baranov could claim the credit for the company's prosperity. Nikolay Rezanov, on an 1805 visit to New Archangel, noted, "His name is heard all along the west coast as far as California. The Bostonians [Americans] respect and honor him, and the natives, even in the most distant places, fear him and offer him their friendship."[15]

Yet Baranov lived a simple life. Rezanov commented,

[Baranov] lives in worse conditions than any of us, in a sort of plank iurt [tent], so damp that the mildew has to be wiped off every day. . . . Once I found his bed standing in water and asked him: "Perhaps the wind tore off a board somewhere?" "No," he replied calmly, "it seems to have flowed in under the floor," and went about his business.[16]

"Honest Joe," Astor, and Kamehameha

From the beginning, the seaport town of New Archangel flourished. Baranov had built ships in Russian America as early as 1790. Now ships bearing the company flag sold furs to the United States, the Philippines, Japan, and Hawaii. Foreign ships arrived as early as 1800. Fifty ships a year would enter for trade. Visitors might find half a dozen brigs and schooners moored in the harbor. American traders, particularly those from Boston, were a regular sight. After a while, many of the Russians in the colony referred to all Americans as "Boston men."[17]

European wars engaged much of Russia's resources in the early 1800s. Ships from the mother country to the colony were rare spectacles. Baranov had little choice but to seek necessary supplies wherever and however he could. He sought and found trade—to his great advantage. Baranov had one rule on foreign trade. He would have nothing to do with traders (particularly Americans) who dealt liquor or firearms to the Tlingit. Other than that, almost anything was acceptable.

"Honest Joe" O'Cain, a Bostonian, had come to New Archangel as the mate on a British ship in 1801. The *Phoenix* provided the colony with molasses, sugar, flour, canvas, and other supplies not available in the North American wilderness. The Russian-American Company discouraged Baranov from buying supplies from foreign merchants. But where were the Russian supply ships? He could not wait forever for their arrival.

O'Cain returned two years later, on his own ship. This time the wily Russian and the ambitious American struck a deal. Baranov would not allow O'Cain to hunt furs in Russian America. But he agreed to lend the services of Aleut hunters so that O'Cain could hunt furs off the California coast. Each Aleut would be paid $2.50 for furs that would fetch ten times as much in the marketplace. It proved profitable for all parties concerned. The 1805 hunt alone brought $250,000 worth of furs.

The Boston man helped the colony in other ways. He brought craftsmen of great skill to Russian America. During one visit, he supplied Baranov with surplus guns and ammunition left over from the American Revolution. These supplies, although old, helped Baranov regain the Sitka fortress from the Tlingit.

O'Cain transported many company furs to the Hawaiian Islands. The islands' king, Kamehameha, appreciated the trade. Whenever a ship sailed from his islands to Russian America, Kamehameha sent pigs, yams, coconuts, taro, or other supplies to his fellow ruler, Baranov. The Hawaiian monarch refused to accept payment for these gifts. The foodstuffs provided by Kamehameha helped sustain the New Archangel settlement in its early years.

Honest Joe O'Cain was not the only American merchant befriended by Baranov. He entered into business agreements with John Jacob Astor, fur trader of the Columbia River. However, he refused Astor's offer to be the sole supplier of goods for the colony.

The War of 1812 between British and Americans caused havoc for American shipping in the Pacific. Baranov took advantage of the chaos. Great Britain dominated the seas; no ship flying an American flag could be considered safe. Baranov bought or leased several American ships, hiring out their crews to do Russian-American Company trading under the Russian flag.

His shrewd moves made a fortune for the company. By the end of 1814, the Russian-American Company had paid stockholders dividends of one million rubles.

The End of Baranov

Despite his success, Baranov was anxious to retire and leave Russian America. He felt the colony would be in good hands with his assistant, Ivan Kuskof. "This place has made me old before my time," Baranov wrote in a letter to company officials.[18] Yet he did not appear destined for retirement. Rezanov talked him out of leaving the colony during his 1805 visit. Later, two different successors left Russia for the colony to replace Baranov. Both died en route.

Events in the colony increased Baranov's unease. A group of colonists in 1809 sought to unseat Baranov.

Aleksandr Baranov, the first and most famous governor of the Russian America colony, ruled for nearly twenty years.

They planned to kill him, seize a ship, sail to Easter Island in the middle of the Pacific, and set up a republic there. Baranov got word of the plot and quashed the uprising. But he never felt secure in New Archangel again. He even sent his family to Kodiak Island for their own safety.

The colony's overall prosperity also hurt Baranov. The Russian Navy, seeing Russian America's progress, wanted control over the colony when the company's charter expired in 1819. Naval officials used their influence with Czar Alexander I to replace Baranov with Leontin Andreanevich Hagenmeister.

A ship commanded by Hagenmeister arrived in New Archangel in 1817. Baranov knew Hagenmeister and disliked him intensely. On a mission to Hawaii, Hagenmeister had behaved arrogantly and foolishly in front of Baranov's friend, King Kamehameha.

Now Hagenmeister was back in New Archangel—and he had secret orders to oust Baranov. The seventy-year-old governor had heard rumors to that effect, but did not believe them. After all, he had built twenty-four outposts and increased the Russian Empire's size and power.

Hagenmeister brought along an auditor to check the financial accounts of the colony. Baranov refused to show the auditor his records, saying that he would do so only under orders from his successor. At that point, Hagenmeister finally showed Baranov the papers stating that he was in charge. Baranov yielded the records; the auditor found not one penny out of place.

There was nothing for Baranov to do now but leave the colony. He was old, tired, and, because of his generosity to Russians and natives alike, nearly penniless. Perhaps he would go to Hawaii and live out his years; he had an open invitation from Kamehameha. When Hagenmeister and other naval officers heard that plan, they promised him a company pension if he returned with them to St. Petersburg.

In November 1818, Baranov left Russian America forever. Russian-American colonists, Aleut hunters, and Tlingit chiefs came to bid him farewell. Hagenmeister commanded the ship. Out of spite, he refused to pass by Hawaii. Baranov never got a chance to meet Kamehameha, who died in 1819 as Baranov was crossing the Pacific.

Hagenmeister's ship, however, spent five weeks on the Dutch East Indies island of Batavia (Java). The intense tropical heat was too much for the aged Russian Baranov. Five days after leaving Batavia, Aleksandr Baranov died and was buried at sea. For the most famous and legendary figure of the Russian America colony, it was an inglorious ending.

7

"BOUND TO SPREAD OVER... AMERICA"

Robert Gray sailed his ship, the *Columbia*, toward China. Before 1790, trade between the United States and China had not been successful. The American colonies had provided little that China wanted. This time would be different. The *Columbia*, an American ship, was carrying a load of furs from the Pacific Northwest. The *Columbia*'s 1790 trip would prove to be more than successful. Chinese merchants craved furs and paid well. Other voyages followed. A typical ship with a load of furs might yield two hundred thousand dollars.

The young American republic dominated the northwest Pacific fur trade from 1790 until 1815, because European powers were involved in a series of wars. After 1815, Great Britain increased its trading in the area. Both the United States and Great Britain spelled unwanted competition for the Russian-American Company.

The Monroe Doctrine

Czar Alexander I started his reign as a liberal. He made many changes in his nation's social structure. He allowed a free press, built universities, and permitted foreign travel. It even appeared that he might free Russia's 20 million serfs from their slavelike existence.

Years of warfare seemed to change his mind. Instead of continuing as a reformer, Alexander turned into a reactionary, someone who opposed change. He muffled the press and activated the secret police. When Latin American nations became independent from Spain, he openly supported Spain's attempt to regain the former colonies. His change of attitude also showed in policies involving Russian America. New opposition to the company occurred in part because some company members had allied themselves with a group called the Decembrists that sought to overthrow him.

When he began his reign in 1801, Alexander did not oppose open trade between the colony and other nations. But he renewed the Russian-American Company's charter in 1821. Immediately afterward, he delivered a bombshell. Russian America's ports would be closed to foreign ships. No foreign ships would be allowed within a hundred miles of the Alaska coast. The czar's ukase also declared the Russian America's southern boundary to be 51 degrees north latitude.

For years, American traders had sold guns and alcohol to the Indians, and for years, the Russians had protested to the American government. The American government had done nothing. The ukase was the czar's way of showing his displeasure.

John Quincy Adams, the American secretary of state, reacted quickly. "[President James Monroe] . . . has seen [the ukase] with surprise," he commented in an understatement.[1] Inside, Adams was seething. He had known the czar when he had served as ambassador to Russia in 1808. He had befriended the ruler and discussed foreign affairs during walks with him. Adams had written his mother, Abigail, that the only hope for a stable Europe lay "upon the moderation, equity, and humanity of the Emperor Alexander."[2] How could this emperor betray the United States?

Adams let the Russian foreign minister know that the ukase was unacceptable to the United States. He claimed that if any American ship were detained for straying inside the Russians' hundred-mile limit, "the excitement in the country will be very great."[3] Adams warned that if anyone would expand territory on the Pacific coast, it would be the Americans.

The decree did something that seemed impossible. It united the Americans and the British on an issue. Both nations, separately, went to St. Petersburg to negotiate with the Russians.

The American government issued a warning in December 1823. During a message to Congress, President James Monroe declared that the United States would not meddle in Old World affairs, but warned European powers to stay out of the Western Hemisphere. Existing colonies would be respected, but "the American continents are henceforth not to be considered as subjects for future colonization by any European power," declared the Monroe Doctrine.[4] In other words: Russia and Spain had better not try to regain the former Spanish colonies.

By itself, Monroe's statement meant little. The United States lacked the military muscle to enforce such a doctrine. But Great Britain, which possessed the

John Quincy Adams was secretary of state during the Monroe administration. Adams was responsible to a large extent for the issuing of the Monroe Doctrine.

world's strongest navy, backed the Americans. Great Britain traded with certain ports in Latin America, which had formerly been closed by the Spanish government, and wanted those ports kept open for British merchants.

United States protests might have startled the Russians. But the effect of the ukase upon the Russian-American Company prompted a treaty. The foreign trade ban was ruining Russian America's economy. Instead of getting necessary supplies from American or other traders, the colony had to wait for Russian ships. These ships took a year to reach New Archangel from Baltic Sea ports. Each trip from Russia cost about three hundred thousand rubles.

Russia and America signed a treaty in 1824. It set the southern boundary of Russian America at 54 degrees, 40 minutes north latitude. Russia would build no new ports outside of the Russian America colony. The countries allowed freedom of navigation to each other. Settled areas could be visited only with the

---

SOURCE DOCUMENT

. . . THE OCCASION HAS BEEN JUDGED PROPER FOR ASSERTING, AS A PRINCIPLE IN WHICH THE RIGHTS AND INTERESTS OF THE UNITED STATES ARE INVOLVED, THAT THE AMERICAN CONTINENTS, BY THE FREE AND INDEPENDENT CONDITION WHICH THEY HAVE ASSUMED AND MAINTAIN, ARE HENCEFORTH NOT TO BE CONSIDERED AS SUBJECTS FOR FUTURE COLONIZATION BY ANY EUROPEAN POWERS. . . .[5]

The Monroe Doctrine warned European powers to discontinue its practice of setting up colonies in the Western Hemisphere.

consent of the local authorities. The United States would prohibit sale of liquor or firearms to natives and would punish offenders. However, Russia had no right to search or seize American ships to look for such illegal goods.

It was a total victory for the Americans. Even the clause limiting trade with the natives meant nothing, because the Russians had no way to enforce it. Adams realized the treaty was a sign of Russian weakness. He predicted that Russian domain would not last long on the northwest coast. "The world shall be familiarized with the idea of considering [America's] proper domain to be the continent of North America," he wrote.[6]

The 1824 treaty was scheduled to last for ten years. After that time, Russia tried to bar United States fishing vessels from Russian-American waters. The United

States refused to go along with this ban. The Russians could do nothing.

Russian-British Relations

A year after the United States, Great Britain signed a treaty with the Russians. This 1825 pact was similar to the American treaty. It gave the British some free trading rights along the North American coast. British ships gained rights to travel on rivers that flowed into the Pacific Ocean.

The treaty also set Russian America's boundaries with Canada. In the southeastern section known as the Panhandle, crests of the coastal mountain range formed the boundary. To the north, the eastern boundary was set at 141 degrees west longitude.

By the 1830s, the Russians decided to cancel the British treaty. However, the British had not violated the agreement. There was no legal reason to break the pact. Russia decided to create a reason. Under the existing agreement, Hudson's Bay Company ships could travel up the Sitkine River. They did not need permission, because there was no settlement there.

Russian-American Company Governor Ferdinand von Wrangell decided to build a settlement, known as Fort Dionysius, at the mouth of the Sitkine. He ordered its commander to forbid the British from entering the river. A British ship, the *Dryad*, tried to pass. The commander of the settlement refused permission. The British ship's captain reported the incident. Great Britain's government filed a 250,000-ruble lawsuit.

Diplomacy won. The Hudson's Bay Company, owner of the ship, dropped the suit. Instead, the Russian-American Company leased the southern part of the colony to Hudson's Bay Company for ten years.

At first, the price of the lease was two thousand sea otter pelts a year. Later, the Russians changed the lease. The British would provide beef, grains, fruits, and other supplies instead of pelts. The British would also supply manufactured goods on demand. The lease was important for the Russians. It decreased their dependence on American ships and traders.

Failure at Fort Ross

Russian America could not survive on furs alone. Settlers needed food, and this food had to come from somewhere. Not even Kamehameha's generous gifts could feed them. New Archangel lay half a world away from St. Petersburg. Ships from there did not arrive on a regular basis. The overland route was not easier. It was three thousand miles to Petropavlovsk and another three thousand to the Siberian city of Irkutsk.

During his 1806 visit to North America, Nikolay Rezanov had visited California. He found a spot about thirty miles north of San Francisco that appeared good for settlement. It had pastureland, timber, running water, and "the best climate on the coast."[7] Aleksandr Baranov went along with the idea.

Baranov's top assistant, Ivan Kuskof, went to Bodega Bay to deal with the local Indians. He paid "three blankets, two axes, three hoes and an assortment of beads" for the site.[8] Kuskof and his men then built a settlement. On August 30, 1812, they raised the Russian flag there.

Fort Ross (originally called Fort Russ, after Russia) became the most imposing fortress in Pacific North America. Its redwood logs could stop anything less powerful than a cannonball. More than forty mounted guns scared away would-be invaders. Fort Ross contained a two-story barracks, two warehouses, officers' quarters, a kitchen, and a blacksmith shop.

Before this colony, no Europeans had settled on the California coast north of San Francisco. Spain had claimed the entire coastal region, but its government could not enforce that claim. Spain was busy fighting France in the Napoleonic wars. France had even invaded its Spanish neighbor. Besides, Spain had trouble elsewhere in the Americas. From Mexico to Central and South America, former Spanish colonies declared independence from the mother country.

Spanish colonial governors in California issued formal protests to Kuskof about the Fort Ross colony. Each time, the answer was the same. Kuskof told the Spaniards to take their problems to Baranov. Then Baranov had told them to bring up their complaints with company headquarters in St. Petersburg. In truth, the protests were a formality. The Spaniards took advantage of the Russian colony. Spanish ships, engaged in warfare elsewhere, were not going to California. The Californians obtained goods from Fort Ross that they could not get at home. Russians, in turn, got food from the Spaniards.

Fort Ross proved to be a failure. In less than ten years, the meager sea otter supply was depleted.

Attempts at shipbuilding proved unsuccessful. The colonists used wood before it was thoroughly dried, with dire results. Spaniards introduced cattle to the colony, but those cattle frequently strayed, ending up as food for predatory animals, Indians, or Spaniards. Likewise, agriculture failed. The Russians and Aleuts who accompanied Kuskof were hunters, not farmers. Fort Ross colonists tried growing wheat, with little success. Soon the colony, which was founded to provide food for Russian America, was itself importing food from its southern neighbor. From 1825 until 1829, Fort Ross's upkeep cost 224,171 rubles. Receipts amounted to only 43,858 rubles.

The Russian-American governor, Ferdinand von Wrangell, visited Fort Ross in 1833. He wrote a pessimistic report to the Russian-American Company's board of directors. Nothing could save the colony except increased trade with now independent Mexico. The Mexican governor hinted that he might give Fort Ross more land if the Russian government recognized Mexico's independence. However, Czar Nicholas I, who came to power in 1825, refused to recognize the independent former Spanish colonies.

When the Hudson's Bay Company agreed to supply Russian America with food, the decision was clear. It was time for Russian America to rid itself of the worthless California settlement. Who would buy it? The Hudson's Bay Company was not interested, nor was the United States. Finally, in 1841, a Swiss immigrant named John Sutter bought the property for thirty thousand piastres (Swiss currency).

In 1848 gold discovered at Sutter's Mill would lure thousands of Americans to California. Fear of these migrants in their territory helped prompt Russia to sell the North American colony. But for now, John Sutter enabled Russian America to rid itself of a nuisance settlement. For the moment, Sutter was a hero.

Elegance, Misery, and Disappearing Furs

Baranov's departure changed the whole personality of New Archangel. No longer was it run by an earthy, rough-and-ready businessman. Later governors, many of them navy men, were honorable and dignified. Social standing was a more important factor for selection of a governor than business sense.

New Archangel became a town that tried to rival St. Petersburg in sophistication. American trader William Heath Davis described the town's ruling class as "highly educated, refined in manners, intelligent and courteous. Most of the gentlemen spoke French and English in addition to their own language."[9] This upper class threw dinner parties and balls or attended amateur theater productions. By 1830, Sitka housed a Russian Orthodox cathedral and various military installations. An imposing structure called Baranov's Castle housed the governor.

For the common workers, however, life was less than perfect. They worked twelve-hour days. Pay was inadequate, and prices at the company store remained high. The Tlingit, although living in a village outside New Archangel, remained a cause for worry. George Simpson, director of the Hudson's Bay Company, called New Archangel the most miserable place he had ever visited.[10]

Many factors worked against the colony. New Archangel was thousands of miles from major Siberian cities, and even farther from St. Petersburg. Transportation within the colony was poor. Land transportation was virtually nonexistent.

Worst of all, the reason for the colony's existence was disappearing. Sea otters, which had numbered in the millions when the Russians arrived, were being hunted to extinction. Ferdinand von Wrangell, the scientist who became governor in 1830, started a conservation program. He divided the colony into districts and prohibited hunting in certain districts in alternating years. His policy did little good. What Russians and their Aleut hunters did not hunt, Americans did. American traders, dealing with natives, removed valuable furs from the Russian colony. From 1821 until 1862, Russians took only fifty-one thousand sea otter pelts—less than one third of the total during the Baranov years. Despite these problems, Czar Nicholas I renewed the Russian-American Company's charter in 1844.

Whales, Coal, and Possibly Gold

Treaties or not, other nations seldom respected Russian America's territorial rights. If Great Britain or the United States wanted to travel or trade in Alaska, they did so without fear of punishment. The Hudson's Bay Company moved through the interior of northwestern North America, including lands west of 141 degrees west longitude. A Hudson's Bay Company party followed the Arctic coast westward to Point Barrow, completing the exploration of Alaska's coastline.

American ships moved freely in Russian-American waters. The Russians could do nothing about them. The ten-year agreement allowing American navigation on Russian inland waters had expired in 1834. The Russian government tried to cancel that part of the 1824 treaty when the treaty ended. William Wilkins, United States ambassador to Russia, warned that if Russia tried to block American ships, the United States might close its ports to Russian vessels.

Whaling ships were the main violators. Oil created from whale blubber fueled lamps. Whalebones were used for anything from needles to women's corsets. By 1834, three hundred whaling vessels hunted off the American coast. Alaskan hunting grounds produced about 60 percent of the oil obtained by the American whaling fleet. One Russian-American captain in 1842 reported spotting at least thirty whaling ships in the Bering Sea alone. The captain asked the Russian government for help. Russia's foreign minister replied that "whalers can be kept from landing, but not from whaling."[11]

American whalers even neared Siberia, hunting off the Sea of Okhotsk. Rather than fight the Americans, Russians decided to compete with them. The government, subsidized by the Russian-American Company, formed the Russia-Finland Whaling Company in the early 1850s. The short-lived company folded in 1854.

Mineral as well as animal resources attracted American interest. The age of wind was giving way to the age of steam on ocean waters, as steam-powered boats began to replace sailing ships. These new ships required coal for fuel.

Whaling ships invaded Russian-American waters, and the Russians could do little to stop them.

Russian America had a large bed of coal on Kodiak Island. At first, the company was reluctant to sell coal to the Americans. The United States, however, was determined to get the vital mineral. The government hinted to the Russians that if the United States did not have free access to Russian-American coal, the United States would charge fees to Russian ships entering American ports. Russians, not wanting to pay high docking fees, dealt coal to the Americans.

Perhaps more than anything else, the Russian-American Company feared discovery of gold on its soil. The United States defeated Mexico in a war and gained the California territory in 1848. Discovery of gold that year lured more than eighty thousand people there in less than two years.

In 1852 a native chief at Queen Charlotte Island, just south of Russian America, showed a yellow rock to a Hudson's Bay Company official. It was gold. This discovery set off another swarm of prospectors. Eight boats carrying several hundred gold seekers came to the British-held island. They depleted the gold supply rapidly and left the island.

Four years later, prospectors found gold in Canada's Fraser River. This discovery led to another gold stampede. Nearly thirty thousand miners fled California for the Fraser River in early 1858. More than gold lured settlers, mainly Americans, to move west. Thousands streamed to the Oregon Territory, just north of California, looking for land. Americans and British had claimed joint control of Oregon since an 1818 treaty. As a result, the United States strengthened its claims to the Pacific Northwest. A boundary dispute nearly led to war between the two nations.

These events frightened Russian-American officials. Even rumors that the Mormons, a religious group, might form a colony in Russian America sent a shiver through company officials. The company probably could not stop the Mormons, much less greedy gold seekers. Americans could soon outnumber the few Russians who lived in the country. If the American government decided to protect its citizens by annexing the Russian America colony, Russians lacked the military power to do anything but protest.

"We Shall Have to Surrender Our North American Possessions"

Russia found better news across the Pacific Ocean. The 1840s found China in troubled times. When the Chinese government tried to halt British shipment of the illegal drug opium into their country, the British declared war. The easy British victory in the Opium War crippled the Chinese. They were forced to pay damages. Great Britain forced the Chinese to open ports for trade. Soon other European nations (although not Russia) received trading privileges.

The Opium War meant two things for Russia. The indebted Chinese nation had little money to buy furs. And the lower-quality furs that the Chinese bought were not acceptable to Europeans or Americans. Thus the main product of the Russian-American Company, already being depleted by overhunting, was of less and less value.

More important, the Russians saw an opportunity and took it. They seized the territory north of Asia's Amur River and set up farms on its fertile land. In 1860 they built Vladivostok, a port at the mouth of the river.

They needed Vladivostok, because a major Siberian port had been destroyed. From 1854 until 1856, Russia fought Great Britain in the Crimean War for control of Black Sea ports. The Russian-American Company and Hudson's Bay Company agreed to neutrality in the European conflict. However, British and French ships attacked the Siberian coast in 1855. They shelled and destroyed the harbor of Petropavlovsk and captured a Russian-American Company ship. This attack, in addition to crippling a port, showed a major weakness. If Russia could not protect its Siberian settlements, how could it hope to defend those in North America? The Crimean War proved a financial hardship to the already burdened Russian government. More and more, it seemed that a North American colony was a luxury Russia could not afford.

Russia needed money to pay its war debts. The United States, a growing and energetic nation, might be willing to purchase Russian America. Nikolai Muraviev, a military official in charge of settling the Amur valley, suggested that Russia turn Russian America over to the United States before Britain could get it. He noted that the newly acquired Asian lands should be Russia's major concern. Muraviev also wrote: "The United States are bound to spread over the whole of North America . . . Sooner or later, we shall have to surrender our North American possessions."[12]

A SCHEMER, A SAINT, AND A PIRATE

Life in Russian America during the nineteenth century might not have been luxurious for most residents, but few could deny that it was interesting. Colorful characters in and around the colony hatched get-rich-quick plans all over the Pacific. There were schemers, pirates, and even an occasional saint.

Russian America's Hawaiian Scheme

The Hawaiian Islands were unknown to Europeans before British Captain James Cook discovered them in 1778. He named them the Sandwich Islands, after the English earl who was Lord of the Admiralty (naval director). Within two decades, these mid-Pacific islands became a major stop for ships of many nations. Ships flying British, Portuguese, French, Spanish, and American flags stopped there. They offered furs and picked up food and sandalwood, a fragrant tree whose bark was made into perfumes and soap. Crews enjoyed a few days' rest in the warm sun.

Kamehameha, king of the island of Hawaii, welcomed these traders. His military power earned him the nickname "Napoléon of the Pacific."[1] But the monarch was also an intelligent ruler who encouraged

Kamehameha, Hawaii's most famous king, considered himself a good friend of Aleksandr Baranov and other Russian officials.

his subjects to learn navigation and allowed them to sign on as crew members aboard foreign ships. Kamehameha was particularly friendly to Baranov. He let Baranov know that he would "gladly send a ship every year, with swine, salt, batatas [sweet potatoes], and other articles of food if they would in exchange let him have sea otter skins at a fair price."[2]

British and American traders wished to set up outposts on Kamehameha's islands. The ruler was not cooperative. He feared that foreign colonization might mean eventual invasion. While Kamehameha gladly allowed visitors, he refused permission from any nation to establish a permanent settlement on his land.

Like other nations, Russia also wanted the islands as a mid-Pacific base. Baranov sent Russian naval officer Leontin Hagenmeister to Hawaii to deal with Kamehameha. The move backfired. Hagenmeister's arrogant behavior annoyed the Hawaiians. After he left, Kamehameha sent a letter to British King George III, seeking a protectorate (treaty of protection) over the islands. The British king declined the offer.

The Russian-American Company, nevertheless, continued trade in the islands. In 1814 the ship *Bering* wrecked near the coast of Kauai. Kaumualii, a foe who wished to conquer Kamehameha, ruled this island.

Baranov saw the accident as a chance for gain. He sent German-born botanist Egor Schaffer to Hawaii to seek damages for the ship. While he was there, he could negotiate for a permanent base. Baranov, however, did not deal with Kamehameha directly. He sent Schaffer on an American ship, the *Isabela*. He told Schaffer not to reveal his real mission until Russian-American

Company ships followed him. Schaffer met the Hawaiian king and introduced himself as a scientist. The generous Kamehameha welcomed him and built a home for him.

Schaffer did not follow Baranov's instructions. He went to Kauai and made his own agreement with Kamehameha's enemy, Kaumualii. On July 1, 1816, they signed a secret treaty. Kaumualii gave Schaffer, through the company, permanent rights to a trading station on Kauai. He also granted Schaffer a monopoly

SOURCE DOCUMENT

1. KING KAUMUALII WILL DELIVER TO THE RUSSIAN AMERICAN COMPANY WHATEVER CARGO OF THE WRECKED SHIP BERING AS HE WAS ABLE TO SALVAGE.

2. KING KAUMUALII PROMISES TO TRADE EXCLUSIVELY WITH THE RUSSIAN AMERICAN COMPANY. IN CASE OF AMERICAN WARSHIPS, HE IS TO SELL TO THEM ONLY PROVISIONS.

3. THE KING SHALL ALLOW THE COMPANY TO ESTABLISH FACTORIES EVERYWHERE IN HIS POSSESSIONS AND HE WILL AID WITH HIS MEN IN THE ERECTIONS OF HIS BUILDINGS AND IN THE DEVELOPMENT OF PLANTATIONS.

4. THE KING WILL FURNISH PROVISIONS FOR ANY RUSSIAN VESSEL . . . IN SIX MONTHS THE CARGO SHOULD BE READY AND THE COMPANY [WILL] UNDERTAKE TO SUPPLY THE KING WITH A FULLY ARMED SHIP.[3]

This contract between King Kaumualii and Egor Schaffer was signed in 1816.

of the island's sandalwood and agreed to "refuse to trade with citizens of the United States."[4] In return, Schaffer promised ships and arms to the Kauai ruler.

This treaty was made without the knowledge, much less the approval, of the Russian-American Company. Baranov, who enjoyed a friendship with Kamehameha, would have been furious with it. Schaffer tried to avoid dealing with the Russian-American colony's governor. He sent a copy of the treaty to St. Petersburg—not on a company ship, but on an American ship, which would send it from China. He asked for quick approval of the treaty, and "to have sent here from St. Petersburg two good ships with reliable crews, well armed."[5]

Kamehameha soon got word of these dealings. *Isabela* crew members, who feared the United States might lose trading rights in Hawaii, warned the Hawaiian leader about Schaffer. Kamehameha, still more powerful than Kaumualii, ordered the Kauai king to remove Schaffer. Kaumualii refused. Word also came to Hawaii from St. Petersburg. The Russian-American Company wanted nothing to do with Schaffer's renegade diplomacy.

In early 1817, six American soldiers and a native chief seized Schaffer. They placed him on an outgoing ship and ordered him away. It meant the end of a Russian-American threat to King Kamehameha's rule. Kamehameha did not believe that Baranov was responsible for this affair. But Schaffer's ill-advised venture also meant the end of hopes for a Russian-American settlement in Hawaii.

"Good Father"

Not every visitor to Russian America went there for money. One of the most honored residents of the colony was interested in souls, not rubles.

Ivan Popov, born in Irkutsk in 1797, entered a seminary at age nine. He soon took the name Ioann Veniaminov. When he graduated, he volunteered to go to Russian America. The Russian Orthodox Church did not force its priests to minister in the colonies. Veniaminov welcomed the challenge and went to Russian America in 1823.

The Russian-American Company offered him the right to sell furs to the natives he served. He declined, saying, "a simple, sincere, and without any remuneration [pay], teaching of Faith would impress people more effectively than the same teaching remunerated by donations."[6]

Father Veniaminov settled on the Aleutian island of Unalaska. He brought his family, plus books, tools, and scientific instruments. Veniaminov found only a run-down chapel on the island. Within two years, he had helped the natives build a new church. In doing so, he gave the Aleuts valuable lessons in carpentry, bricklaying, and metalworking. His school taught homemaking skills to girls, house building to boys.

Veniaminov learned from the natives, and he taught them as well. He wrote an Aleut dictionary, grammar book, and primer. He translated gospels, sermons, and a history of the local church. Half a century later, an Aleut woman recalled, "When he preached the Word of God, all the people listened, and listened without moving, until he stopped. Nobody thought of fishing or hunting while he spoke; nobody felt hungry or thirsty as long as he was speaking, not even little children."[7]

Ioann Veniaminov was a man of science as well as a man of God. He maintained a weather observatory while studying plant, mineral, and animal life. He invented a sundial watch and a clock that ran from dripping water. He talked with natives and recorded their stories. Natives told him about incidents as far back as the decades-old Soloviev massacre. He published these studies as a book, *Notes of the Islands of the Unalaska District*. Several articles he wrote were translated into French and German.

Veniaminov became bishop of Russian America and eastern Siberia. After ten years in Unalaska, Veniaminov transferred to New Archangel. He soon befriended the Tlingit there. During a smallpox epidemic, which wiped out a quarter of

Father Veniaminov served Russians settlers and natives throughout the Russian America colony. He later became the leader of the Russian Orthodox Church.

the Tlingit population, he sent medicine to natives throughout the colony.

Veniaminov had the largest missionary field in the world. He spent four months a year traveling by kayak or dogsled to distant outposts. When not traveling, he built St. Michael's Cathedral. The church, with its copper spire, gold and white interior, and religious artifacts, was the religious jewel of Russian America. Veniaminov built four other new churches, including one in Siberia, plus thirty chapels.

After more than thirty years in Alaska, he left for the final time to head the diocese in Yakutsk, Siberia.

St. Michael's Cathedral (its interior seen here) was the religious center of the Russian America colony.

In 1868, he was named metropolitan of Moscow, the highest position in the Russian Orthodox Church. He served as metropolitan until his death in 1879.

One traveler described the hefty priest as "quite herculean and very clever."[8] Another, comparing him to a legendary American lumberjack, called him "Paul Bunyan in a cassock [priest's robe]."[9] Natives had a more affectionate name for him. They simply called him "Good Father."[10]

Confederate Pirates in Alaska

Alaska lay thousands of miles from the United States, but the last shots of America's Civil War were fired there. A Confederate pirate ship, the *Shenandoah*, fired those shots.

The *Sea King* was launched from a Glasgow, Scotland, shipyard in 1863. It carried British troops to New Zealand, then returned home. Early the next year, Confederate agent James Bullock agreed to buy it. The ship sailed from London in 1864 flying the British flag, then met Bullock at an island in the middle of the Atlantic. When the transaction was completed, the renamed *Shenandoah* sailed to Australia. Along the way, it captured several American ships.

While the *Shenandoah* was docked in Australia, the American government demanded that Australia's territorial governor seize the ship for "piratical acts."[11] The governor did nothing, and the Confederate ship headed northward in early 1865.

The *Shenandoah* left a trail of terror in its wake. Commander James Waddell raided American ships, capturing their cargoes and destroying the ships. He did this in the belief that the Civil War was still being fought, though the war had ended in April.

In mid-June, the *Shenandoah* entered the Bering Sea whaling grounds. On June 22, the Confederate maverick captured the *William Thompson* and the *Euphrates*. Others in the Arctic whaling fleet also fell. Commanders of the destroyed ships told Waddell that the war was over. He would not believe them.

On August 2, Waddell encountered a British ship. Its commander convinced him of the Civil War's end. The Confederate captain wrote in the *Shenandoah* log, "Having received by the British barque [boat] 'Barracouta' the sad intelligence of the overthrow of the Confederate Government, all attempts to destroy shipping or property of the United States will cease from this date."[12] Waddell sailed back to safety in Great Britain, avoiding coasts and possible attacking ships along the eleven-thousand-mile route.

The *Shenandoah* had captured more than thirty American ships worth more than a million dollars, taking 1,055 prisoners. The Russian-American Company, aware of this raider in its waters, was powerless. If the company could not stop a renegade ship from a defunct nation, how could it hope to repel an organized invasion from European or American navies? It seemed one more argument that the colony must be sold.

9

THE PURCHASE OF "SEWARD'S FOLLY"

Captain P. N. Golovin had discovered gold in Alaska's Copper River in 1860. This should have been a cause for joy. Instead, it was a cause for caution. The officials of the Russian-American Company at first denied the gold rumors, and then called them exaggerated. The company even appealed to St. Petersburg for a warship to drive away a possible army of prospectors. That crowd of gold seekers never appeared. But the Russian-American Company already had its share of problems.

"All the Financial Resources . . . Could Hardly Be Sufficient"

Theater dates and dinner parties continued in Sitka in the early 1860s. But the Russian-American Company had seen better times. Fur seals, hunted nearly to extinction, were beginning to recover their previous numbers. But other commercial ventures proved short-lived. The Russian-American Company no longer sold coal and ice to Americans in the recently admitted state of California.

The Russian-American Company's charter expired at the end of 1861. Czar Alexander II appeared in no hurry to renew it. He sent Golovin and Councilor of State Sergei Katlitsev to report on the colony's progress. Their report was less than glowing.

Golovin and Katlitsev's report questioned the security of the colony. The report criticized the company for making no effort to explore the interior. It noted that the Tlingit "tolerate the Russians" but added that "if they were to unite under the leadership of a brave chief, the Kolosh [Tlingit] would easily conquer our settlements and kill all the Russians."[1] Golovin noted that the colony had potential mineral riches, but the company did little to exploit them.

The report did not recommend abolishing the company. However, it called for massive changes in the colony's government. The company should retain its fur monopoly, but nothing else. The Russian America colony should have a court system and a governor appointed by the Crown. Individuals there should live and work where they pleased. Class distinctions should be abolished. The Russian-American Company directors refused these recommendations.

Tempers flew during the lengthy hearings to determine the company's future role.[2] Russian America was an expensive proposition. The government paid the company two hundred thousand rubles a year to maintain the colony—and this was during peacetime. The report recommended that the Russian Crown take over the government of the colony. If it did so, costs to the government would skyrocket. The investigating commission concluded that "all the financial resources of [Russian America] could hardly be sufficient to repay the expenses of its defense or even simple administration."[3] Yet the government, while not renewing the charter, did not let the company fold.

These hearings destroyed the company. Its status was uncertain. It could not obtain much-needed loans. Most important, the hearings revived rumors that the Russian government was planning to sell the colony.

Selling the American Colony

Alexander II had ambitious ideas when he assumed power in 1855. The thirty-two-year-old czar planned to free the serfs, overhaul the courts, ease censorship, allow independent universities, and create local and provisional governments. These reforms required money, and money was in short supply. Russia's disastrous defeat in the Crimean War had drained the economy.

Fortunately for Alexander, there was a potential source of income. Russian America lay untouched after the Crimean War. Great Britain could have taken the lightly guarded colony with little struggle. Alexander's brother, Grand Duke Constantin, was a major navy official. He noted that if Great Britain did not try to take the colony one day, the United States would. "We must not deceive ourselves," he wrote Russia's foreign minister, Prince Aleksandr Gorchakov. "The United States, aiming constantly to round out their possessions and desiring to dominate undividedly the whole of North America, will take the aforementioned colonies from us and we shall not be able to retain them."[4]

Gorchakov, one of Europe's leading statesmen, saw no "political necessity" for selling the American colony.[5] However, he did not necessarily want to keep it forever. He might favor selling Russian America—if the price was right.

During the Crimean War, California Senator William Gwin paid Edouard de Stoeckl a call. Gwin told the Russian ambassador that he had heard that Russia needed money. Would Stoeckl's government be interested in selling its American territories?

Stoeckl reported to Alexander that he favored a sale of the North American lands. His voice joined those of Constantin and former colonial governor Ferdinand von Wrangell. But before the countries could negotiate a sale, events in the United States intervened.

"Thank God for the Russians"

The issue of slavery had divided the American nation for decades. When Abraham Lincoln was elected president in 1860, the divisions opened wide. Eleven southern states seceded (withdrew) from the Union. They declared themselves the Confederate States of America. It would take a civil war to reclaim them.

European nations watched American events with great interest. Silently or openly, most hoped for a Confederate victory. Europe's nations would be at an advantage when dealing with divided American states. They could have a military and economic edge over two weaker nations rather than one strong one.

The Union had one solid ally—Russia. The two large nations had similarities. President Lincoln freed American slaves. Czar Alexander freed his nation's serfs. Russians and Americans also had had little conflict with each other. Alexander commented, "The Russian and American peoples have no injuries to forget or remember."[6]

In 1863, the Russian Navy sent its fleet to the United States. Ships stopped at New York and San Francisco. Thousands of people, including President Lincoln, visited them. The Russians never gave an official reason for the tour, but the message was clear. European nations should stay out of American affairs. Do not attempt to evade Union blockades of Confederate ports. The United States was grateful for this action. Secretary of War Gideon Welles wrote in his diary: "Thank God for the Russians."[7]

The Civil War ended with a Union victory in April 1865. There were no immediate talks about a sale of Russian America. But the Russians looked forward to working with the United States and its president, Abraham Lincoln.

"Arrogant, Brilliant, Sometimes Devious"

John Wilkes Booth gathered his would-be assassins together. The famous actor sympathized with the recently defeated Confederacy. He hated President Lincoln. Booth felt there was still hope for his defeated nation. He and his partners would destroy the United States by killing its most important leaders. These included Lincoln, Vice President Andrew Johnson, and Secretary of State William Seward.

Booth sneaked into Washington's Ford Theatre and shot the president. A few hours later, Abraham Lincoln was dead. The men assigned to assassinate Johnson and Seward were not so successful. Johnson's would-be killer lost his nerve, got drunk, and never saw the vice president. Seward was injured by his attacker but survived.

These events proved vital to the purchase of Alaska. Perhaps Lincoln would have approved the purchase of the gigantic territory, but the Civil War put more important matters on his mind. His successor, Andrew Johnson, showed little interest either way in buying the Russian colony. He would let his Cabinet make the decision for him.

Secretary of State William H. Seward had no such hesitation. Indeed, he seldom showed indecisiveness during his political life. He was described as "arrogant, brilliant, sometimes devious."[8] His strong antislavery views made him a leader in the young Republican party. He had sought the party's presidential nomination in 1856 and 1860, losing both times. President Lincoln named him to the most important Cabinet position, secretary of state.

Lincoln had chosen Democrat Andrew Johnson as his vice-presidential running mate in 1864. He hoped that putting the Tennessee Unionist on the ticket might help win the election. After Johnson became president, he showed sympathy toward the recently defeated South. His leniency infuriated many ruling Republicans. They would make his term in office a continuous nightmare.

Seward remained loyal to the new president. His cooperation with Johnson cost him dearly. Political allies in his native New York deserted him. His national reputation soured. But he still held the position of secretary of state. He would make the most of it.

William Seward, United States secretary of state, was the driving force behind the American purchase of Alaska.

William Seward believed in Manifest Destiny. To him, the United States had the right and responsibility to control the northern part of the North American continent. He wanted Russian America from the Russians, as well as Greenland and Iceland from Denmark.

Seward desired the largely unknown territory for more than the natural riches it might contain. By purchasing Russian America, Seward hoped to prevent Canada from moving toward a confederation (union of separate provinces). Then the United States might obtain western Canada's British Columbia territory as well. In early 1867, Johnson's Cabinet, with the president sitting quietly through the meeting, approved the purchase of the Alaska territory. Now all Seward had to do was convince the Russians.

A Clever "Papa"

Edouard de Stoeckl first came to the United States in 1841. The thirty-three-year-old gentleman stayed for more than twenty-five years. Americans liked and respected the elegant Stoeckl. They gave him the nickname "Papa."[9]

Even so, Stoeckl probably welcomed his 1866 transfer to the Netherlands. No more would he have to suffer the hot, humid, mosquito-ridden summers of Washington, D.C. Now he could relax in the refined atmosphere of Amsterdam, a pleasant European capital. First, however, he went to St. Petersburg.

While at the Russian capital, Stoeckl gave the opinion that the Americans might want to buy Russian America. Constantin heard Stoeckl's views and contacted his brother, Czar Alexander. Stoeckl,

Constantin, Gorchakov, and the czar discussed the possible sale. Alexander asked Stoeckl to return to the United States and make a deal. Stoeckl, perhaps seeing his plum Netherlands assignment flying away, had little choice but to agree.

Stoeckl arrived in New York in February 1867. Through a mutual acquaintance, he contacted the secretary of state. Seward was willing to talk, but he demanded total secrecy. Stoeckl soon found out why. He learned that there might be congressional opposition to a purchase. Stoeckl wrote Gorchakov: "This opposition is not aimed at the 'transaction' itself as from the passionate animosity which reigns in the Congress against the President and even more against the secretary of state."[10] Stoeckl volunteered to talk with influential Congress members. Seward opposed that idea. If anyone would talk to the congressmen, he would do it.

Stoeckl had orders not to accept less than $5 million for the territory. Seward offered that amount. Stoeckl stalled; he thought he could get more. Five and a half million, Seward offered. He said that was his final offer, because the Cabinet would not approve a purchase at a higher price. Again Stoeckl held out; he wanted $7 million. Seward agreed. It was the price he had originally planned on offering. Stoeckl hesitated again. Seward threw in an extra $200,000, and the Russian agreed to the deal.

Stoeckl contacted Russia's foreign office in St. Petersburg. A telegraph dated March 28 ordered him to complete the transaction.

A "Dark Deed Done in the Night"

William Seward was at home chatting with friends on Friday night, March 29, 1867. He was expecting no other visitors. A knock on the door interrupted the gathering. It was Stoeckl. He had received permission from the czar to conclude the treaty. Would Seward be willing to meet tomorrow at the State Department to discuss the treaty?

Seward did not want to wait. The Senate was scheduled to end its session at noon the following day. He wanted to introduce the treaty before it adjourned. Seward told Stoeckl, "If you can muster your legation together before midnight, you will find me waiting for you at the Department, which will be open and ready for business."[11]

Stoeckl, Seward, and their staffs gathered to iron out the treaty. The two diplomats provided a contrast. Stoeckl was "a large man, large of face and figure, quite unconventional, and with easy, pleasant manner."[12] Seward, on the other hand, was "a slouching, slender figure" with

Edouard de Stoeckl, Russia's ambassador, felt he got a good deal with the Russian America sale.

"a beaked nose; shaggy eyebrows; unruly hair and clothes . . . and a perpetual cigar."[13] But they had a common goal. They wanted the sale of Russian America to the United States, and they wanted it as soon as possible.

At four o'clock in the morning, they concluded the treaty. Russia would turn over its American lands after the Senate voted the treaty's approval. There was no time for sleep. Seward hurried to the Capitol to present it to the Senate. He knew that he lacked the votes to pass the treaty. But if he could get the Senate to call a special session to consider the treaty, he would get those votes later.

Seward got the needed time. Senators grumbled as President Johnson called an "extraordinary occasion" of the legislative body.[14] Most had little interest in some unknown, barely mapped territory thousands of miles away. They resented having to vote on a treaty they considered a "dark deed done in the night."[15] Perhaps most important, they hesitated to do anything that might be seen as an accomplishment by their foe, Andrew Johnson.

Through early April, the nation held a lively debate over whether to buy the territory. Those who favored the purchase pointed out its many advantages. They said that such a purchase might make it easier to acquire Great Britain's Pacific territories. It might also help open up trade to the Orient. It could help maintain good relations with the czar and Russia. Cassius M. Clay, minister to Russia, sent congratulations for a brilliant treaty, "which adds so vast a territory to our Union; whose ports, whose mines, whose waters, whose furs, whose

William Seward (seated), Edouard de Stoeckl (at globe), and their aides worked all night on March 29, 1867, to create the Alaska purchase treaty.

fisheries are of untold value."[16] Given these advantages, the Boston *Herald* noted in an editorial, the price for Russian America was "dog cheap."[17]

Others had different views. Newspaper publisher Horace Greeley charged that Johnson was using the purchase to take people's minds off the country's problems at home. *Harper's Weekly* claimed the purchase might cause bad relations with Great Britain. The New York *World* claimed "Russia has sold us a sucked orange. . . . It has ceased to be of any use to Russia."[18] The *New York Tribune* termed the purchase "Seward's Folly" or "Johnson's Polar Bear Garden."[19] Some had mixed views. The *New York Post* called the land a "frozen sterile desert" in its first edition but later favored the purchase.[20] The *New York Herald* humorously called it "Walrussia" (walrus-inhabited Russia) but asked for a favorable vote.[21]

Stoeckl and Seward picked up one very important ally. Charles Sumner, chairman of the Senate Foreign Relations Committee, studied all available literature on Russian America. Then he presented an impassioned, three-hour speech to his fellow senators. "Perhaps no region of equal extent, unless we accept the interior of Africa or possibly Greenland, remains so little known," he admitted.[22] But he told his fellow senators that it had

> forests of pine and fir waiting for the axe . . . coal and copper, if not iron, silver, lead, and gold . . . the two greatest products of New England, granite and ice . . . fisheries which, in waters superabundant with animal life beyond any of the globe, seem to promise a new commerce.[23]

He told them he favored the purchase, not just for the land's wealth, but to show United States friendship for Russia. Finally, he proposed a new name for Russian America—the Aleut name, Alaska.

Sumner needed to use all of his oratorical skills to gain acceptance of the purchase. Treaties require a two-thirds vote of the Senate. Twenty-six out of the thirty-nine senators had to favor it. The purchase passed with twenty-seven votes—only one to spare. When Sumner requested that the vote be made unanimous, two senators dissented.

Any celebrations by Sumner, Seward, or Stoeckl were premature. The purchase of Alaska faced one more major hurdle.

"Under No Obligation to Vote Money"

The Senate could approve a treaty to buy foreign territory. But that approval meant nothing without the money necessary to buy it. That appropriation (permission to spend the money) had to come from the House of Representatives. And the House was in no hurry to cough up money for some Arctic ice palace.

House Majority Leader Thaddeus Stevens assured Stoeckl that the House would pass the appropriation soon. Even though Stevens was a bitter enemy of Johnson, he promised action during the House's July session. July passed, and nothing happened. August and September went by with no vote. American troops raised the Stars and Stripes at Sitka on October 18, 1867. There was still no sign that the Congress back home would agree to pay for the land these troops were now occupying.

Meanwhile, Russians were becoming edgy about the lack of action by the United States. Many in Russia opposed the sale anyway. Some found it shameful that Russia was yielding its hard-won territory. Ministers found it sinful that natives would be deprived of the Orthodox faith. The Russian-American Company realized it would go out of business once the territory was transferred. Company officials protested the sale, but the protests did little good. Russia's ministers answered critics by claiming the treaty would cement friendship with the United States. Ironically, diplomats of each nation tried to persuade hesitant foes to accept the sale because they claimed the other country wanted it.

The House had a reason for its delay. That reason had little to do with mineral wealth, polar bears, or icebergs. Andrew Johnson remained president—but, it appeared, not for long. Members of Congress appeared ready to vote him out of office. Meanwhile, they would not do anything that would put him in a favorable light. Representative Cadwalader E. Washburn of Wisconsin even proposed a resolution against the purchase. This resolution said the House was "under no obligation to vote money to pay for any such purchase unless there is greater present necessity for the same than now exists."[24]

Johnson sweated through 1867 and 1868. The charges against him were purely political—the Republican-dominated Congress wished to remove him for not acting according to its wishes. Most of the charges against him stemmed from Johnson's wishes to replace certain Cabinet members—a right routinely granted to previous presidents. However, there were enough votes to remove him from office if Congress members voted along party lines. The House voted 126 to 47 to impeach (bring accusations against) the president on February 24, 1868. Now the case went to the Senate, where a two-thirds vote would convict him, and remove him from office. On May 16, James Grimes of Iowa had to be carried into the chamber on a stretcher. He gasped a vote for the president. It came down to the last senator. If Edmund Ross voted guilty, Johnson would be convicted by a 36 to 18 vote. If Ross moved to acquit the president, Andrew Johnson would be saved by one vote. When he was asked, "How say you?" the young Kansas Republican

Andrew Johnson, United States president, showed little interest in the Alaska purchase. He was more concerned with his struggle against Republican members of Congress.

answered "Not guilty."[25] Ross correctly predicted that this deciding vote would ruin his political career. "I looked into my open grave," he remarked.[26]

With the 35 to 19 vote, Johnson remained in office. But he had no real power. He would be merely serving out his term. His foes realized Johnson's weakness. His bills could pass now, but he was too politically weak to get advantage from them.

After the acquittal, Stoeckl and Seward set to work. They mounted a furious propaganda campaign detailing the advantages of the Alaska purchase. They hired lobbyists, including Robert Walker, the former treasury secretary. Walker earned his pay. He bombarded the

SOURCE DOCUMENT

THE POSSESSION OF THIS COUNTRY IS OF NO VALUE . . . TO THE UNITED STATES . . . THAT IT WILL BE A SOURCE OF WEAKNESS INSTEAD OF POWER, AND A CONSTANT ANNUAL EXPENSE FOR WHICH THERE WILL BE NO ADEQUATE RETURN . . . NO CAPACITY AS AN AGRICULTURAL COUNTRY . . . NO VALUE AS A MINING COUNTRY . . . ITS TIMBER . . . GENERALLY OF POOR QUALITY AND GROWING ON INACCESSIBLE MOUNTAINS . . . ITS FUR TRADE . . . OF INSIGNIFICANT VALUE AND WILL SPEEDILY COME TO AN END . . . THE FISHERIES OF DOUBTFUL VALUE. . . .

THE RIGHT TO GOVERN A NATION . . . OF SAVAGES IN A CLIMATE UNFIT FOR THE HABITATION OF CIVILIZED MEN WAS NOT WORTHY OF PURCHASE.[27]

The Minority Report of the House of Representatives Committee on Foreign Relations was not very enthusiastic about the purchase of Alaska.

Washington *Chronicle* with articles describing Alaska's abundant fisheries and mineral wealth.

The appropriations bill came to the House floor in June 1868. Two weeks of long, emotional debate followed. Supporters quoted Sumner's speech and favorable newspaper editorials. Opponents left no doubt or criticism unspoken. One representative suggested giving Russia the purchase price and telling them to take back the colony. Some had questions about Alaska's value. But they felt it would be dishonorable to go back on a deal already made.

When the vote came, the total was not close. On July 14, 1868, the purchase passed 113 to 43, with 44 abstentions. Even this lopsided vote had its doubters.

Many foes of the purchase pictured Alaska as a wasteland filled with glaciers.

Some Congress members and newspapers charged that Stoeckl and Seward had used bribery to assure the pro-purchase vote. These questions surfaced in August. Stoeckl received $7.2 million for Alaska, but only $7.065 million of that money made it to Russia.

What happened to the remaining $135,000? Seward denied that he had paid any bribes. But he dodged questions on whether his Russian counterpart had done so. Stoeckl admitted he had paid three thousand dollars to the owner of Washington and Philadelphia papers that supported acquisition, and another thousand dollars to a California newsman. However, he refused to testify before a Senate committee that was investigating the bribery charges. Walker admitted he had received twenty thousand dollars for his services. He added, "I told [Stoeckl] I had never lobbied Congress in my life, and that I never meant to, and if he wished me to lobby Congress generally I must decline."[28]

The investigating committee made a halfhearted effort to investigate the bribery charges. In the end, it found nothing. However, it appears that money might have been paid for votes. Years after Andrew Johnson's death, a note was discovered, written in his handwriting. In it, he claimed that Seward had told him bribery had been used to influence approval of the purchase of the Alaska territory.[29]

On October 18, 1867, the United States gained control of Alaska. But what did Americans really acquire? Alaska was the second largest land purchase in history. Only the Louisiana Purchase was larger. The Alaska territory measured more than 586,000 square miles. Its coastline was longer than that of the entire United States. But

BOOMS, BUSTS, AND BASES

little of the country had been explored. Russians had held military control only over the town of Sitka. Thousands of miles of mountains, forests, and plains had been unseen by Europeans or Americans.

Russian America had never held more than nine hundred Russian settlers. Now, many of them were leaving. The cession treaty allowed Russians to remain in the territory for three years. After that, they could choose to become American citizens or leave. With the Russian-American Company disbanded, most had no jobs. They could not get work with the United States military. A few stayed, some went to California or British Columbia, but most returned to Russia.

A new set of immigrants replaced them. Americans streamed to Sitka, hoping to find some kind of wealth. They included real estate dealers, miners, homestead seekers, and those looking for fortunes by legal or illegal means. Sitka became a lively town, boasting restaurants, saloons, and even two bowling alleys. The boom lasted only a year or so. Those late arrivals left as quickly as they came.

That migration did not disturb William Seward. In 1870, someone asked him what was his greatest accomplishment as a politician. He answered without hesitation, "The purchase of Alaska! But it will take the people a generation to find that out!"[1]

Seward's Treasure Chest

A generation after Seward's remark, the American people found out about Alaska's riches. News of gold brought a stampede of miners to the Bering Sea outpost of Nome in 1900. The Nome discovery was hardly the first gold strike in Alaska. The Panhandle

SOURCE DOCUMENT

I HAVE LOST MYSELF IN ADMIRATION FOR SKIES ADORNED WITH SAPPHIRE AND GOLD AS RIGHTLY AS THOSE WHICH ARE REFLECTED IN THE MEDITERRANEAN. OF ALL THE MOONLIGHTS IN THE WORLD, COMMEND ME TO THOSE WHICH LIGHT UP THE ARCHIPELAGO OF THE NORTH PACIFIC OCEAN.

THE ENTIRE REGION OF OREGON, WASHINGTON TERRITORY, BRITISH COLUMBIA, AND ALASKA SEEM THUS TO BECOME A SHIP YARD FOR THE SUPPLY OF ALL NATIONS.[2]

William Seward, pleased with his purchase of Alaska, made this speech at Sitka on August 29, 1869.

town of Juneau had had a gold rush in 1880. But that rush was small compared with the thirty thousand people who flocked to Nome at the turn of the twentieth century. Miners found more than $2 million worth of gold the first year and $4 million a year for several years after that.

Prospectors found other gold sites. A mining settlement on the Tanana River would become the city of Fairbanks. But for the most part, the boom did not last. World War I and the end of the gold strikes drove most immigrants to other places.

Even without a large population, Alaska remained important to the United States. At the time of the purchase, Illinois Representative Green B. Raum predicted,

> The day will come when the Pacific will be our greatest stronghold, and when that day arrives, those responsible for the building and maintaining of the necessary defense depots will bless the memory of those whose courage and foresight have caused them to vote for the confirmation of this treaty.[3]

The congressman's words were prophetic. Alaska was a strategic defense center against Japan in World War II. During the Cold War, in which the Russia-dominated Soviet Union posed a threat to American security, Alaska's bases provided a guard against Arctic or Pacific invasions.

World War II prompted construction of the Alaska Highway. This land route through Canada linked Alaska with the "Lower 48" states. After the war, tourists and adventurous spirits traveled the highway. Some decided to stay in Alaska. They were joined by

Gold miners streamed to Alaska in the 1890s, seeking their fortunes.

military personnel who enjoyed their stays at Alaska bases. These immigrants helped swell Alaska's population. Congress granted Alaska statehood in 1959.

Alaska has had its share of busts, but there have also been booms. Only a handful of people lived within a thousand miles of the Arctic Ocean's Prudhoe Bay in 1967. Geologists, however, discovered a sea of petroleum under the nearby land. The North Slope oil field contains an estimated 9.6 billion barrels of oil and 26 trillion cubic feet of natural gas. A thousand-mile-long pipeline carries the petroleum to the southern port of Valdez. From there, tankers carry it all around the world.

Without a barrel of oil or cubic foot of natural gas, Alaska would still be considered a bargain. Even before statehood, Alaska had produced a fortune in natural resources. The annual value of its fishing industry surpasses those of all other states. Lumber, gold, coal, sand, and gravel are among many materials shipped elsewhere from the northwest giant.

Seward's Folly, indeed!

★ TIMELINE ★

1728—Vitus Bering passes through Bering Strait.

1741—Alexei Chirikov, a commander of Bering's second expedition, sights Alaskan land; Bering's crew, wracked with scurvy, is shipwrecked off the island that now bears his name; Bering dies.

1743—First promyshlenniki fur-hunting expedition.

1749—Ministers under Czarina Elizabeth begin system of collecting tribute in furs from Aleuts.

1762—Aleut revolt results in four destroyed Russian ships; Russian retaliation takes thousands of Aleut lives.

1774—Spaniards explore Northwest coast, including area near Sitka.

1778—Captain James Cook's third Pacific expedition maps Alaska's southern coast but fails to find Northwest Passage.

1784—Grigory Shelekhov establishes the first white settlement at Three Saints Bay on Kodiak Island.

1799—Aleksandr Baranov establishes a settlement a few miles north of present-day Sitka; Czar Paul grants a twenty-year renewable charter to the Russian-American Company.

1802—Tlingit massacre all but a few inhabitants of Sitka settlement.

1804—Baranov, accompanied by Russians and Aleuts, drives Tlingit from settlement, and establishes New Archangel at Tlingit Sitka site.

1812—Russian-American Company establishes Fort Ross settlement at Bodega Bay.

1815 —Egor Schaffer fails to set up Russian-American
–1817 settlement in Hawaii.

1821—Ukase issued by Czar Alexander I forbids foreign trade in Russian America, leading to protests by British and Americans; Russian-American Company gets second charter.

1823—Monroe Doctrine warns Europe not to interfere with independent American nations.

1824—Father Ioann Veniaminov begins ministry in Russian America; Russians and Americans agree to treaty allowing free trade in Russian ports by American ships; Treaty recognizes 54 degrees, 40 minutes north latitude as southern Alaska boundary.

1825—British and Russians sign treaty allowing British free trade and setting Russian boundaries.

1840—Hudson's Bay Company leases southern part of Russian America colony.

1841—Russians sell Fort Ross to Swiss immigrant John Sutter.

1854 —Crimean War points out Russian military weakness
–1856   in Pacific Ocean.

1865—Confederate raider *Shenandoah* sinks American ships off Alaska coast.

1867—United States Senate approves treaty for purchase of Alaska; Russians give up Russian America on October 18.

1868—House of Representatives appropriates money for Alaska purchase.

1900—Discovery of gold near Nome attracts thirty thousand prospectors.

1959—Alaska becomes America's forty-ninth state.

1967—Geologists discover widespread oil deposits near Prudhoe Bay.

★ Chapter Notes ★

Chapter 1. "We Now Stood on American Soil"

1. Ernest Gruening, *The State of Alaska: A Definitive History of America's Northernmost Frontier* (New York: Random House, 1968), p. 25.

2. Archie W. Shiels, *The Purchase of Alaska* (College, Alaska: University of Alaska, 1967), p. 150.

3. Hector Chevigny, *Russian America: The Great Alaskan Venture 1741–1867* (Portland, Oreg.: Binfords and Mort, 1965), p. 256.

4. Quoted in Henry Steele Commager, ed., *Documents of American History*, 6th ed. (New York: Appleton-Century-Crofts, Inc., 1958), vol. 2, pp. 42–43.

5. Ronald Lautaret, *Alaskan Historical Documents Since 1867* (Jefferson, N.C.: McFarland and Company, 1989), p. 8.

6. Ibid., p. 9.

7. Editors of Time-Life Books, *The Alaskans* (Alexandria, Va.: Time-Life, 1977), p. 57.

Chapter 2. Early Life in "The Great Land"

1. Polly Miller and Leon Gordon Miller, *Lost Heritage of Alaska: The Adventure and Art of the Alaskan Coastal Indians* (Cleveland, Ohio: The World Publishing Company, 1967), p. xiv.

2. Hilary Stewart, *Looking at Totem Poles* (Vancouver: Douglas and McIntyre, 1993), p. 9.

3. Claus M. Naske and Herman E. Slotnik, *Alaska: A History of the 49th State* (Norman: University of Oklahoma Press, 1987), p. 18.

4. Cora Cheney, *Alaska: Indians, Eskimos, Russians, and the Rest* (New York: Dodd, Mead, 1980), p. 12.

Chapter 3. In Search of "Soft Gold"

1. M. A. Groushko, *Cossack: Warrior Riders of the Steppes* (New York: Sterling Publishing Co., 1992), p. 70.

2. Ibid., p. 38.

3. Valentin Rasputin, *Siberia, Siberia* (Evanston, Ill.: Northwestern University Press, 1991), p. 41.

4. Quoted in Rasputin, pp. 43–44.

5. Quoted in W. Bruce Lincoln, *The Conquest of a Continent: Siberia and the Russians* (New York: Random House, 1994), p. 57.

6. Hector Chevigny, *Russian America: The Great Alaskan Venture 1741–1867* (Portland, Oreg.: Binfords and Mort, 1965), p. 18.

7. Robert Wallace, *Rise of Russia* (Alexandria, Va.: Time-Life, 1967), p. 156.

8. Henri Troyat, *Peter the Great*, trans. Joan Pincham (New York: E. P. Dutton, 1987), p. 154.

Chapter 4. "Discover America"

1. Cora Cheney, *Alaska: Indians, Eskimos, Russians, and the Rest* (New York: Dodd, Mead, 1980), p. 30.

2. John David Ragan, *The Explorers of Alaska* (New York: Chelsea House Publishers, 1992), p. 34.

3. Cheney, p. 4.

4. Ragan, pp. 34–35.

5. W. Bruce Lincoln, *The Conquest of a Continent: Siberia and the Russians* (New York: Random House, 1994), p. 106.

6. Quoted in Ernest Gruening, *The State of Alaska: A Definitive History* (New York: Random House, 1968), p. 11.

7. Cheney, p. 39.

8. Ragan, p. 39.

9. Ibid., p. 40.

10. Quoted in Ernest Gruening, *An Alaskan Reader, 1867–1967* (New York: Meredith, 1966), p. 4.

11. Ragan, p. 40.

12. Ibid., p. 40.

13. Polly and Leon Gordon Miller, *Lost Heritage of Alaska: The Adventure and Art of the Alaskan Coastal Indians* (Cleveland, Ohio: The World Publishing Company, 1967), p. 17.

14. Quoted in Ragan, p. 43.

15. Clifton Daniel, editorial director, *Chronicle of America* (Fairbrough, Hampshire, England: JOL International Publishing, 1993), p. 102.

16. Gruening, *The State of Alaska*, p. 15.

Chapter 5. Exploitation, Not Partnership

1. W. H. Pierce, *13 Years of Travel and Exploration in Alaska 1877–1889* (Anchorage: Alaska Northwest Publishing Co., 1977), p. 38.

2. William Coxe, *The Russian Discoveries Between Asia and America* (Ann Arbor, Mich.: University Microfilms, 1966), p. 31.

3. Quoted in Clarence C. Hulley, *Alaska: Past and Present* (Portland, Oreg.: Binfords and Mort, 1970), p. 62.

4. Hector Chevigny, *Lord of Alaska: Baranov and the Russian Adventure* (Portland, Oreg.: Binfords and Mort, 1951), p. 12.

5. Hector Chevigny, *Russian America: The Great Alaskan Venture 1741–1867* (New York: Viking Press, 1965), p. 48.

Chapter 6. The Age of Baranov

1. Quoted in William R. Hunt, *Alaska: A Bicentennial History* (New York: W. W. Norton, 1976), pp. 24–25.

2. W. Bruce Lincoln, *The Conquest of a Continent: Siberia and the Russians* (New York: Random House, 1994), p. 136.

3. Quoted in Ernest Gruening, *An Alaskan Reader, 1867–1967* (New York: Meredith, 1966), p. 20.

4. Hector Chevigny, *Russian America: The Great Alaskan Venture 1741–1867* (Portland, Oreg.: Binfords and Mort, 1965), p. 91.

5. Clarence C. Hulley, *Alaska: Past and Present* (Portland, Oreg.: Binfords and Mort, 1970), p. 118.

6. Henry W. Clark, *History of Alaska* (New York: MacMillan, 1930), p. 53.

7. Gruening, p. 19.

8. P. A. Tikhmenev, *A History of the Russian American Company* (Seattle: University of Washington Press, 1978), p. 12.

9. Quoted in William R. Hunt, *Alaska: A Bicentennial History* (New York: W. W. Norton & Co., 1976), p. 27.

10. Quoted in Morgan B. Sherwood, ed., *Alaska and Its History* (Seattle: University of Washington Press, 1967), p. 88.

11. Aurel Krause, *The Tlingit Indians: Results of a Trip to the Northwest Coast of America and the Bering Straits* (Seattle: University of Washington, 1956), p. 29.

12. Chevigny, p. 96.

13. David Wharton, *They Don't Speak Russian in Sitka: A New Look at the History of Southern Alaska* (Menlo Park, Calif.: Markgraf Publications Group, 1991), pp. 6–7.

14. Quoted in Sherwood, p. 52.

15. John David Ragan, *The Explorers of Alaska* (New York: Chelsea House Publishers, 1992), p. 60.

16. Tikhmenev, pp. 89–90.

17. Wharton, p. 5.

18. Chevigny, p. 93.

Chapter 7. "Bound to Spread Over . . . America"

1. Morgan B. Sherwood, ed., *Alaska and Its History* (Seattle: University of Washington, 1967), p. 89.

2. Howard I. Kushner, *Conflict on the Northwest Coast: American-Russian Rivalry in the Pacific Northwest 1790–1867* (Westport, Conn.: Greenwood, 1975), p. 45.

3. Ibid., p. 50.

4. Ernest Gruening, ed., *An Alaskan Reader, 1867–1967* (New York: Meredith, 1966), p. 98.

5. Quoted in Henry Steele Commager, ed., *Documents of American History*, 6th ed. (New York: Appleton-Century-Crofts, Inc., 1958), vol. 1, p. 236.

6. Quoted in Kushner, p. 46.

7. Vladimir Wertsman, ed., *The Russians in America: A Chronology and Fact Book* (Dobbs Ferry, N.Y.: Oceana Publications, 1977), p. 43.

8. Clarence C. Hulley, *Alaska: Past and Present* (Portland, Oreg.: Binfords and Mort, 1970), p. 140.

9. Editors of Time-Life Books, *The Alaskans* (Alexandria, Va.: Time-Life, 1977), p. 19.

10. Quoted in Claus M. Naske and Herman E. Slotnik, *Alaska: A History of the 49th State* (Norman: University of Oklahoma, 1987), p. 57.

11. Quoted in Kushner, p. 88.

12. Hector Chevigny, *Russian America: The Great Alaskan Venture 1741–1867* (Portland, Oreg.: Binfords and Mort, 1965), p. 223.

Chapter 8. A Schemer, a Saint, and a Pirate

1. Richard A. Pierce, *Russia's Hawaiian Adventure 1815–1817* (Berkeley: University of California Press, 1965), p. 2.

2. Quoted in Pierce, p. 2.

3. Ibid., p. 64.

4. Ernest Gruening, ed., *An Alaskan Reader, 1867–1967* (New York: Meredith, 1966), p. 75.

5. Hector Chevigny, *Russian America: The Great Alaskan Venture 1741–1867* (Portland, Oreg.: Binfords and Mort, 1965), p. 158.

6. Morgan B. Sherwood, ed., *Alaska and Its History* (Seattle: University of Washington, 1967), pp. 125–126.

7. Chevigny, p. 200.

8. Editors of Time-Life Books, *The Alaskans* (Alexandria, Va.: Time-Life, 1977), p. 36.

9. Ibid.

10. Sherwood, p. 129.

11. Ibid., p. 191.

12. Ibid., p. 199.

Chapter 9. The Purchase of "Seward's Folly"

1. Basil Dmytryshyn and E. A. P. Crownhart-Vaughan, *The End of Russian America: Captain Pavel Nikolaevich Golovin's Last Report 1862* (Portland, Oreg.: Oregon Historical Society, 1979), p. 27.

2. Hector Chevigny, *Russian America: The Great Alaskan Venture 1741–1867* (Portland, Oreg.: Binfords and Mort, 1965), p. 236.

3. Howard I. Kushner, *Conflict on the Northwest Coast: American-Russian Rivalry in the Pacific Northwest 1790–1867* (Westport, Conn.: Greenwood Press, 1975), p. 138.

4. Chevigny, p. 234.

5. Ibid., p. 233.

6. Clarence C. Hulley, *Alaska: Past and Present* (Portland, Oreg.: Binfords and Mort, 1970), p. 199.

7. Chevigny, p. 237.

8. Editors of Time-Life, *The Alaskans* (Alexandria, Va.: Time-Life, 1977), p. 41.

9. Chevigny, p. 224.

10. Quoted in Kushner, p. 144.

11. Editors of Time-Life, p. 43.

12. Albert Castel, *The Presidency of Andrew Johnson* (Lawrence, Kans.: Regent's Press of Kansas, 1979), p. 120.

13. Editors of Time-Life, p. 42.

14. Castel, p. 121.

15. Editors of Time-Life, p. 43.

16. Ernest Gruening, *The State of Alaska: A Definitive History of America's Northernmost Frontier* (New York: Random House, 1968), p. 24.

17. Kushner, p. 146.

18. Archie W. Shiels, *The Purchase of Alaska* (College: University of Alaska, 1967), p. 2.

19. Castel, p. 121.

20. Kushner, p. 145.

21. Ibid.

22. Ernest Gruening, ed., *An Alaskan Reader, 1867–1967* (New York: Meredith, 1966), p. 38.

23. William R. Hunt, *Alaska: A Bicentennial History* (New York: W. W. Norton, 1976), p. 33.

24. Morgan B. Sherwood, ed., *Alaska and Its History* (Seattle: University of Washington, 1967), pp. 235–236.

25. Clifton Daniel, editorial director, *Chronicle of America* (Fairbrough, Hampshire, England: JOL International, 1993), p. 406.

26. Richard B. Bernstein and Jerome Agel, *Of the People, By the People, For the People: The Congress, the Presidency, and the Supreme Court in American History* (New York: Wings Books, 1993), p. 41.

27. Quoted in Gruening, p. 27.

28. Sherwood, p. 248.

29. Chevigny, p. 244.

Chapter 10. Booms, Busts, and Bases

1. John David Ragan, *The Explorers of Alaska* (New York: Chelsea House Publishers, 1992), p. 63.

2. Ellen Lloyd Turner, senior ed., *Alaska: A Chronology and Documentary Handbook* (Dobbs Ferry, N.Y.: Oceana, 1972), p. 55.

3. Archie W. Shiels, *The Purchase of Alaska* (College: University of Alaska, 1967), p. 178.

★ FURTHER READING ★

Books

Cheney, Cora. *Alaska: Indians, Eskimos, Russians, and the Rest*. New York: Dodd, Mead, 1980.

Editors of Time-Life Books. *The Alaskans*. Alexandria, Va.: Time-Life Books, 1977.

Kushner, Howard I. *Conflict on the Northwest Coast: American-Russian Rivalry in the Pacific Northwest 1790–1867*. Westport, Conn.: Greenwood, 1975.

Lautaret, Ronald. *Alaskan Historical Documents Since 1867*. Jefferson, N.C.: McFarland and Company, 1989.

Lincoln, W. Bruce. *The Conquest of a Continent: Siberia and the Russians*. New York: Random House, 1994.

Naske, Claus M. and Herman E. Slotnik. *Alaska: A History of the 49th State*. Norman: University of Oklahoma, 1987.

Ragan, John David. *The Explorers of Alaska*. New York: Chelsea House Publishers, 1992.

Rasputin, Valentin. *Siberia, Siberia*. Evanston, Ill.: Northwestern University Press, 1991.

Troyat, Henri. *Peter the Great*. New York: E. P. Dutton, 1987.

Wharton, David. *They Don't Speak Russian in Sitka: A New Look at the History of Southern Alaska*. Menlo Park, Calif.: Markgraf, 1991.

Internet Addresses

Alaska Department of Education. *Alaska Purchase Centennial Collection: A Historical Survey in Pictures*. n.d. <http://www.educ.state.ak.us/lam/library/hist/cent/home.html>. (June 9, 1999).

National Archives and Records Administration. *The Alaska Purchase Treaty*. n.d. <http://www.nara.gov/education/historyday/alaska/treaty.html>. (June 9, 1999).

★ INDEX ★